The Visitor's Guide
to
CORSICA

D0188016

THE
VISITOR'S GUIDE TO
CORSICA

MPC

HUNTER
PUBLISHING INC

British Library
Cataloguing in Publication Data

May, Jutta
    The visitor's guide to Corsica.—
(Visitor's guides).
    1. Corsica—Description and travel—
1981- —Guide-books
    I. Title II. Korsika. *English*
    914.4'94504838   DC611.C812

Author: Jutta May
Translator: A.J. Shackleton

© Goldstadtverlag Karl A. Schäfer,
    Pforzheim
© Moorland Publishing Co Ltd
    1987 (English edition)

Published by
Moorland Publishing Co Ltd,
Moor Farm Road,
Airfield Estate,
Ashbourne, Derbyshire
DE6 1HD, England

ISBN 0 86190 175 4 (paperback)
ISBN 0 86190 176 2 (hardback)

Published in the USA by
Hunter Publishing Inc,
300 Raritan Centre Parkway,
CN94, Edison, NJ 08818

ISBN 0 935161 17 1

Cover photograph: *Propriano*
(Spectrum Colour Library).
Colour illustrations have been
supplied by Peter Lamb (Ile
Rousse; Calvi; Santa Regina;
Calacuccia; Sant' Antonio;
Algajola and Porto/Piana). The
remainder and the black and
white illustrations were kindly
supplied by the French
Government Tourist Office.

Printed in the UK by
Butler and Tanner Ltd, Frome, Somerset.

CONTENTS

Touring Routes

The old Corsican capital of Ajaccio has been chosen as the starting point. Routes 1 to 4 run clockwise round the coast, passing from one resort to the next, until they eventually arrive back at Ajaccio. The last route goes from Ajaccio through the mountains of the interior.

The Towns and their Surrounding Area

This chapter includes the main tourist centres on Corsica, together with the areas surrounding them. This will give holidaymakers an idea of what is to be seen in the area where they are staying.

Key to Symbols Used in Margin

⌘ Items of cultural or historical interest.

 A beautiful view or interesting natural phenomenon.

INTRODUCTION

1. Geology and Scenery

Geologically speaking, the island of Corsica is a mountain range that rises from the sea bed. Its rocky coastline is washed by the clear waters of the Mediterranean, while in spring and autumn the air is full of the scents of its many flowering plants.

Corsica is the fourth-largest island in the Mediterranean, coming after Sicily, Sardinia and Cyprus. Until recently it was France's largest *département*, with Ajaccio as its capital. But a few years ago it was divided into the two administrative regions of Haute-Corse and Corse-du-Sud. With an area of 8,772sq km, it is a little larger than the English county of North Yorkshire. It is 184km long and 83km wide. The highest point is Monte Cinto, at 2,707m above sea level.

The islands of Corsica and Sardinia form a single geological unit, and are separated by a channel only 11km wide. Corsica is divided from France by 180km of sea, which reaches depths of up to 2,000m. The Italian coast is only half as far away. Corsica is linked to Italy via an undersea ridge which is never more than 180m below the surface, and from which the Tuscan Islands are formed. The largest of these is Elba, only 40km from the Corsican coast.

The higher mountains to the west of the island are formed from a block of ancient crystalline rocks, while the softer sedimentary rocks to the east were folded into mountains at the same time as the Alps. In the south these consist mostly of fissured limestone, which has been eroded to form delightful geometrical patterns. These two main geological regions are divided by a central mountain range that runs in a gentle curve from one end of the island to the other. It forms the backbone of the island, with subsidiary ranges forming 'ribs' on either side.

The two highest mountains are Monte Cinto (2,707m) and Monte Rotundo (2,622m). The latter is part of a massif that includes eleven mountain lakes. The third-highest peak is Paglia Orba (2,525m) — probably the most beautiful mountain in

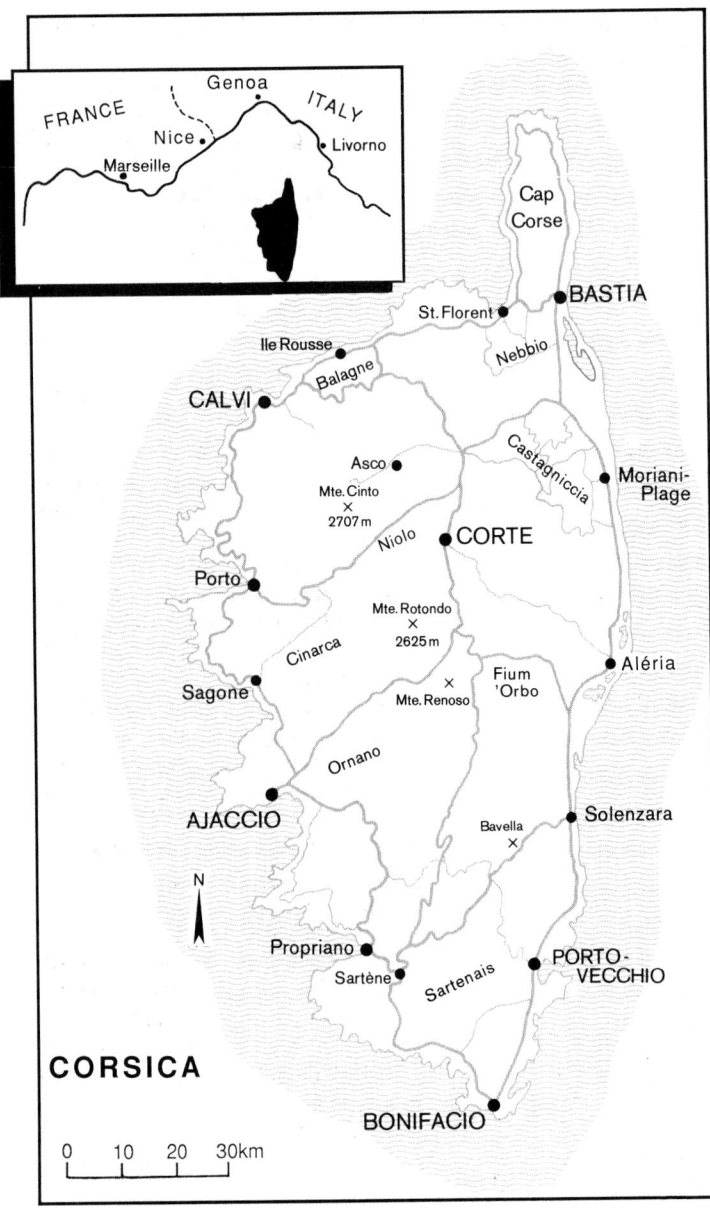

FRANCE

Genoa

ITALY

Nice

Marseille

Livorno

Cap
Corse

St. Florent   BASTIA

Ile Rousse

Balagne   Nebbio

CALVI

Asco   Castagniccia

Mte. Cinto
×
2707 m   Moriani-
Plage

Niolo   CORTE

Porto

Mte. Rotondo
×
2625 m

Cinarca   Fium
'Orbo

Sagone   ×   Aléria
Mte. Renoso

Ornano

AJACCIO   Bavella
×

N   Solenzara

Propriano   PORTO-
VECCHIO
Sartène   Sartenais

CORSICA

BONIFACIO

0   10   20   30km

Corsica. Other peaks include Monte d'Oro (2,389m) and Monte Renoso (2,352m).

The mountain ranges are divided by deep valleys and gorges, which have been carved out of the rock by fast-flowing streams. The result is some quite breathtaking scenery, such as the **Scala di Sta Regina** in Niolo, the **Gorges de Spelunca** near Porto, and the **Gorges de la Restonica** near Corte. Examples among fold mountains to the east are the **Défilé de Lancone** to the south of Bastia and the gorges of the **Fium' Orbo** near Aléria. Many of the valleys lead to remote mountain passes, where the roads often climb to over 1,000m, affording some magnificent views. The highest of these passes is the **Col de Vergio** (1,464m).

The mountains have sometimes been eroded into bizarre shapes. The beautiful **Aiguilles de Bavella**, for example, are reminiscent of the Dolomites, and are a must for all visitors to Corsica. The *tafoni* are yet another interesting rock formation. *Tafoni* is a Corsican word meaning 'holes', and these rocks are indeed full of holes like Swiss cheese. The holes vary in depth, and sometimes form channels right through the rock. For this reason they are often known as 'windows'. The phenomenon has yet to be fully explained, though it is undoubtedly due to erosion.

Corsica is an island of bare peaks and vertical rock faces, and the west coast is similarly precipitous. The steep cliffs of variegated, mostly reddish rock are broken up into numerous inlets and sandy bays, where the green vegetation contrasts with the blue waters and white foam of the Mediterranean. The mountains are less high to the east, and are divided from the coast by a floodplain with long, sandy beaches. To the south the coast becomes steeper and more irregular, forming two large and beautiful bays.

The northern peninsula of **Cap Corse** is of particular interest, forming as it were a microcosm of the whole island. Its highest point is Monte Stello (1,305m), and the most northerly is the island of Giraglia. A road winds and twists all the way round the coast from Bastia to St Florent. It is in some places hewn out of the cliffs, but also passes through orchards and vineyards, and through lovely villages which cluster romantically around the hillsides and bays.

Immediately to the south of Cap Corse is a lush region known as **Nebbio**. The direct road from Bastia to St Florent passes over

Corsica — an island of bare peaks, cliffs and sandy beaches

Lush, green valleys, vineyards and maquis-covered slopes

the Col de Teghime (549m), providing some magnificent views. The Défilé de Lancone provides some outstanding examples of unusual rock formations. The region also includes the famous menhirs of Piève and the beautiful Pisan church of St Michael near Murato. To the north-west is the bare wilderness of the Désert des Agriates.

To the west of Nebbio and inland from Ile Rousse is **Balagne** — a delightful region of lush valleys filled with olive groves. To the south of here the land becomes mountainous. The **Niolo** region is looked on as the true heart of Corsica. This remote mountain valley is surrounded by the island's highest peaks, and was once the exclusive domain of shepherds and crofters. The scenery is wild and beautiful, with forests and steep gorges. The road goes from Corte to Calacuccia, and then crosses to Porto via Corsica's highest pass, the Col de Vergio (1,464m).

East of Niolo and south of Nebbio is the mountainous but populous region of **Castagniccia**, which is bordered to the north and south by the rivers Golo and Tavignano. It owes its name to the chestnut forests which cover the whole area, imbuing it with a special kind of beauty, especially when the leaves turn in November. This area was at the centre of the Corsican struggles against the Genoese, in which the convents of Orezza and Alesani played an important part. Morosaglia was the birthplace of Pasquale Paoli, Corsica's greatest hero, who lost a decisive battle at Ponte Nuovo.

Casinca is the name given to the north-eastern part of Castagniccia together with the coastal floodplain south of Bastia Airport, which was once heavily cultivated by the Romans. It is a region steeped in history, with picturesque old villages perched on the hillsides. It is a paradise for those tourists who prefer to avoid the coastal resorts. On the site of the old Roman settlement of Mariana is the beautiful twelfth-century St Mary's Basilica, known as La Canonica. It is the finest example of its kind on the whole island.

South of Castagniccia is the region of **Fium' Orbo**, which is named after the river of the same name. It is a thinly populated area similar to Niolo, though the mountains are not so high and the climate is drier and warmer. There is a road through the valley, which in several places forms gorges such as the Défilé de l'Inzecca. Forestry used to be the main occupation, but since the 'sixties French Algerian immigrants have been clearing the slopes near the coast to make way for vineyards, orchards and fields.

The south-western part of the island is called **Sartenais** after the small town of Sartène, which is the best-preserved example of a traditional Corsican town. The region is full of fascinating prehistoric sites: temples and menhirs, and the ancient fortifications of the Torrean and Megalithic civilisations. The most important sites are those of Filitosa and Cucuruzzu. The coast is steep and indented, and culminates in the strange chalk cliffs of Bonifacio.

The adjoining region to the north is **Ornano** — the heart of western Corsica, known in French as *au delà* or 'the other side'. Bastelica is of particular interest here, and is within easy reach of Ajaccio. Further north is **Cinarca**, which borders on the Gulf of Sagone. It is an area of lush, green valleys, with vineyards and *maquis*-covered slopes.

Further north again, between Balagne and the Gulf of Porto, is the north-western part of an area which has been designated a nature reserve. This reserve extends through central Corsica to the Aiguilles de Bavella in the south-east, and contains the finest of Corsica's mountain scenery.

Corsica's vegetation is typically Mediterranean

2. Climate and Travel

As befits a Mediterranean island, Corsica enjoys a Mediterranean climate, with mild, wet winters and hot, dry summers. However, this is only strictly true of those parts of the island less than 200m above sea level. In the so-called transitional zone between 200m and 1,000m, the seasonal differences are less marked, while from 1,000m to 1,500m, the climate is temperate. Above 1,500m the climate becomes typically alpine, which means everything other than warm, with fog in the autumn and blizzards in the winter that can come as far down as 300m. Even at the height of summer, the evenings can be cool at sea level, while the mountain regions are liable to occasional storms.

An approximate guide to average air temperatures may be found on page 218. The water temperature reaches its maximum in August (average 25°C, 77°F), dropping to a minimum of 15°C (59°F) during the winter. It slowly warms up during May and June to 19°C (66°F), and gradually cools down during September and October to between 20°C (68°F) and 21°C (70°F).

Rainfall is low in summer and high in winter. It never rains in July or August apart from occasional thunderstorms, and the river beds are partially dried up. In September the heavy showers and thunderstorms begin that are so typical of these latitudes; they let up somewhat during January and February, and become more frequent again in March. They depend very much on the local winds, which are many and varied on Corsica.

In winter the winds are predominantly mild, wet westerlies. They are forced to rise sharply over the mountains, making the rainfall much heavier on the western side. One of the least pleasant of these westerlies is the *libeccio*, which is caused by the wind funnelling down into the valleys on the eastern side. It is often very stormy, and poses a danger to shipping off the east coast, especially around Bastia. Then there is the *mistral* — a cold, dry north-westerly that comes across from France.

The hot, dry *scirocco* that comes up from the Sahara can produce stormy weather in the mountains, especially in the spring. The extreme south of the island is protected from it by Sardinia. The east coast is often affected by the warm, moist *levanter*, which comes across from the east. It sometimes makes the air so unpleasantly sultry that the inhabitants escape to the fresher air of the mountains.

The most pleasant of these winds is the *tramontane* — a fresh, dry wind that comes down from the north, but which is not very common.

Vines among the maquis

In addition to these winds, there are so-called thermal winds that are caused by local changes in temperature. In warm weather the air rises up the valleys during the day, creating a valley breeze, then sinks at night to produce a mountain breeze. Coastal areas develop sea breezes in the morning and land breezes in the evening, providing the coastal vegetation with much-needed moisture.

The best time to travel for bathers and hill-walkers is probably the high summer, when the weather is most reliable. Those visitors who belong to neither of these categories, but can travel at no other time, are advised to avoid the heat and the crowds on the coast, and to stay up in the mountains. One need not go far from the coast, and there are some beautiful places to stay.

Otherwise, spring and autumn can be very much pleasanter. Swimming is still perfectly possible, while ramblers and nature-lovers will not only find the island much quieter, but will also pay less for accommodation. Spring is the time when the *maquis* is in bloom; with its marvellous fragrance, it has a beauty all of its own, which is highlighted by the white of the snow-covered peaks and the blue of the sky. It flowers a second time in the autumn. Thus the more temperate early autumn and late spring (May/June, September/October) are in many ways preferable to the hottest months of July and August. February can also be beautiful — Corsica's 'white spring', when both the white heather of the *maquis* and the fruit trees are in blossom.

3. Flora and Fauna

The vegetation of the island is affected not only by the climate but also by altitude and situation. About three quarters of its area is covered by forests or by the famous *maquis*, and only 15 per cent of it is cultivated.

Up to an altitude of 200m, and sometimes as high as 400m, the vegetation is typically Mediterranean, with trees and plants from all over the Mediterranean, and from other parts of the world that enjoy the same climate: the tamarisk and the fig cactus, the agave and the yucca from America. The Canaries date-palm has become common, especially along the coast, and is even found in Corte. Like the banana tree, it does not produce fruit on Corsica.

Avenues and squares are often shaded by plane and eucalyptus trees. The cemeteries are full of cypress trees, which

Goats and mouflon roam the mountains

often stand guard around remote churches and chapels. The plains and valley slopes are often covered with olive trees, which lend a distinctive silver-grey sheen to the landscape.

One interesting feature, particularly in the south of the island, is the brick-red colour of the cork oak which has been stripped of its bark. The beaches are lined with stone-pines, and the areas nearby are covered with thistles and reddish-coloured mesembryanthemums ('midday flowers'). The island is alive with the bright colours of numerous exotic flowers, whether in gardens and parks, in pots and window boxes, or simply growing wild.

Some of the lower slopes have been painstakingly turned into terraces. These are planted with fruit crops such as peaches, apricots, citrus fruits, pomegranates, figs and vines, vegetables such as artichokes, and also tobacco and grain crops.

The slopes up to 900m are covered with forests of sweet chestnut trees, and fruit trees of the kind found in more northerly climes. The forests up to 1,200m consist mainly of the famous Corsican pine, which can grow as high as 40m. Beech, oak and Scots pine can grow at 1,800m above sea level, while the birches form the actual tree line.

Above that the only trees are the occasional dwarf juniper or alpine alder, and the vegetation consists of grassland with numerous small alpine flowers. At these altitudes the ground can remain snow-covered for 7 to 8 months of the year.

The *maquis*, which grows all over Corsica, is a peculiarly Corsican phenomenon. It was originally the French term for an evergreen shrub known in English as the rock-rose. The generic name is *Cistus*, and there are several different species on the island. On the damper slopes to the west it can grow as high as 4m, whereas in higher or more arid regions its growth remains stunted. The French word comes from the Italian *macchia*, which in turn is derived from the Corsican word *mucchio*.

The word's meaning was extended to include all the associated scrub vegetation, and it took on yet another meaning at the time when outlawed Corsican freedom-fighters went into hiding. Instead of saying that they had been outlawed, people described them as having 'gone off into the *maquis*'. The name was used again during World War II, this time to refer to the French resistance movement.

The beauty of the *maquis* is impossible to describe adequately to someone who has not seen or smelled it. One must simply experience it for oneself. No wonder that there are even special coach trips or '*maquis* tours' laid on!

Spring in Corsica begins as early as February, when the trees come into blossom. At the same time the green *maquis* suddenly turns into a sea of white as the heather comes into bloom. The first shrub to blossom is the pale-lilac rosemary. In March this is joined by the snowball and the yellow-flowered gorse, and the ground becomes carpeted with variegated mosses and grasses.

From mid-April through to mid-June, the *maquis* remains a glorious symphony of colour and fragrance. There are violets and narcissi, orchids and fennel, passion-flowers and geraniums, marguerites and mimosas, tiger-lilies and many more. The shrubs blossom into a medley of colours, including the white, pink and red blooms of the rock-rose, the red-lilac thyme, the greenish-white laurel, the greenish-yellow spurge. There are several different species of broom, including many beautiful yellow-flowered varieties. Then there is the wild asparagus, and the colourful splendour of the oleander and bougainvillaea.

In late May and early June, the wild lavender fills the landscape with splashes of light blue, closely followed by white myrtle flowers and the greenish-yellow oleaster. High up in the mountains there are chamois tufts and small white flowers known as Corsican edelweiss (*Helichrysum frigidum*).

In July and August the agave on the coast raises its yellow 'beacons' towards the sky. Soon after that the autumn blossoms appear. And even the winter remains colourful, with the varied red tints of the aloe flowers.

The *maquis* spreads quickly, and all cultivated land must be carefully protected from it. But it is also beneficial in that like forests it acts as a reservoir of moisture. On the other hand the dead branches and dried-out pine-needles often constitute a severe fire risk in dry weather. They have even been known to ignite spontaneously, and the resulting fires can destroy whole areas of *maquis* and forest.

The Corsican fauna is very much less varied than the flora. The *maquis* and the forests are remarkable for their silence, unless one visits them very early in the morning. The island supports eagles and falcons, and is a popular stopping-off point for birds on their seasonal migrations; but there are very few resident songbirds. Perhaps this is because the Corsicans have exploited them for commercial gain, blackbird pâté being very much a local delicacy.

The only carnivore is the fox. There are supposed to be deer in the forests, but they are very difficult to find. The wild boar are certainly still around, and the *maquis* forms an ideal feeding ground for them. There are plenty of small game such as hares, partridges and squirrels, with tortoises and lizards creeping through the undergrowth. There are adders, which are fortunately not poisonous, and numerous large and exotic species of butterfly and beetle.

The high mountains are inhabited by mouflon — a rare species of wild sheep with gigantic horns. It is even quicker and shyer than the chamois. The mouflon alone is sufficient justification for the existence of a nature reserve on Corsica.

Most of the lakes and mountain streams are full of trout, with eels in their lower reaches. The coastal waters support the usual Mediterranean fish, including sardines, tuna, shrimps and especially lobsters; but the fishing grounds are not very productive. There are mussels and oysters along the beaches and bays of the east coast, but they are collected for pleasure rather than for economic gain.

The pursuit of agriculture is an activity fraught with problems on a barren island such as Corsica, which relies very much on help from outside.

4. The Corsican People

Corsica over the centuries has been a melting pot for the many different races that have invaded the island: Greeks, Carthaginians, Etruscans, Romans, Vandals, Ostrogoths, Saracens, Italians, Spaniards and finally the French. It is therefore not surprising that the Corsican temperament is so varied and so full of contradictions.

The only two traits that all Corsicans possess are their love for their island and their desire for freedom. It is something which they have never lost, and which no occupying power has been able to take away from them. Even today, the French government grants them certain special rights and privileges.

The island has 220,000 inhabitants, of whom 55,000 live in Bastia, the main commercial and industrial centre in the north, while 50,000 live in the southern capital of Ajaccio. In third place, with 6,000 inhabitants apiece, are the three towns of Sartène, Porto-Vecchio and Corte. On the other hand, there are 100,000 Corsicans living in Marseille, which is thus effectively the largest Corsican town.

The island's population peaked at the beginning of this century at 295,000. Since then, especially in recent years, the Corsicans have been leaving their island in droves, often to study for a profession or to join the armed forces. It is usually economic hardship that forces them to leave their beloved homeland, which they affectionately refer to as 'Cursichella' or 'dear little Corsica'. Most of them, however, return in old age.

Most Corsicans have traditionally been fishermen and shepherds, but these occupations are not economically viable these days. Agriculture is increasing, but it is an activity that has never attracted them. The mass exodus has meant that worker shortages have added to the island's problems. However, in spite of the fact that only 15 per cent of the land surface is cultivated, agriculture and forestry are the island's most important economic activities, employing about half of its workforce. There is an emphasis on livestock, which relies almost exclusively on grazing; cattle and pigs are produced for their meat, sheep for cheese, and goats for their milk.

The late 'fifties saw an alarming increase in the number of people leaving the island, and since then there have been strenuous efforts to modernise and increase output in all areas of the economy. But such improvements take time to achieve. There

Corsicans are a warm and hospitable people

are other reasons for these problems, quite apart from the Corsican temperament. One of these is the lack of educational and professional opportunities. For although isolated, the younger generation is more modern in outlook, and craves a much higher standard of living than the island can be expected to provide.

About a fifth of the land surface is covered in forest, and this

Tourism flourishes, but Corsica remains unspoilt

has benefited some of the wood-processing industries. The island's natural resources include asbestos, which until recently was mined on Cap Corse. Also, green slate is quarried near Bastia and marble near Corte. But the transport costs to the mainland are simply too high.

The island has a number of small food industries, but they fulfil only part of its needs, and most commodities must be imported from outside, beer included. Some activities have proved profitable, such as the liqueur industry in Bastia and the production of Roquefort cheese. Also, Corsican honey is renowned for its fragrance. The island's flourishing tobacco industry has provided yet further employment. At harvest time, however, extra workers have had to be drafted in from Italy. The island's exports have so far failed to equal imports, and the result is that the cost of living on Corsica is about 30 per cent higher than on the French mainland.

In 1976 a working party was set up towards the development of tourism, which promises to bring substantial improvements to the life of the islanders. The result has been a building programme of hotels and holiday flats, which alas have sometimes rather spoiled the scenery. The road network has been improved, while houses and restaurants are gradually being renovated.

Corsica is slowly becoming more prosperous, albeit at the cost of its tourist centres losing some of their identity. The success of these developments is reflected in the increased number of charter flights to the island, which people have jokingly referred to as a kind of modern equivalent of pennies from heaven.

It is true that tourism flourishes for only part of the year, and then only in a few coastal resorts. But it is a form of activity that suits both Corsica and its inhabitants. The island boasts some beautiful scenery and a climate that is attractive to tourists, while the Corsicans themselves are a naturally hospitable race. Their hospitality was legendary in the past, when they would willingly take in even enemies if the circumstances dictated.

The vendetta is another important element of Corsica's past. Even today a Corsican family will stay together through thick and thin, but at one time family honour was carried much further. If someone was alleged to have committed a crime against another, then the head of the complainant's family had the right to exact vengeance on the perpetrator by having him killed. This right overrode the judgement of any outside authority, if any such body existed. In those days, if someone was afraid of being made the victim of a vendetta, then he would hide in the *maquis* and become an outlaw. Then it was often a question of joining the 'right' gang of bandits in order to survive. Such activities are now a thing of the past.

The Corsicans come over as a very leisurely and easy-going race, but with a strong sense of honour and pride. If a train or a bus is unexpectedly delayed, they will simply pass the time with a quiet game of *boules*. In the country men can often be seen in the morning sitting quietly smoking their pipes, having already finished a hard day's work. The Corsicans' pride means that there are no beggars on the island. Outside the tourist areas, the tipping of waiters is treated as an insult. A cigarette is the most that one might offer them.

The Corsicans are very fond of music and singing, though the traditional shepherd's pipe, zither and harp have been replaced by the guitar. In the soft light of a balmy summer evening, they will often take up their guitars and burst into song. The tunes are not specifically Corsican in style. Singers on the coast will perform a few well-known modern songs, together with some of the more romantic Italian melodies — fishing songs, love songs and serenades. There are, however, a few Corsican hymn tunes that have become popular outside Corsica. And it is not often realised

Folk dancing for the tourists

that Tino Rossi was a Corsican.

Up in the mountains it is still possible to hear traditional Corsican folk music. It is somewhat Arabic in sound, and in some ways reminiscent of Gregorian chant. It is full of sadness and passion like the Corsicans themselves. It includes, for example, the so-called *chiam' e rispondi* — antiphonal songs which are typically Corsican and often border on the satirical. These are sung on the coast as well, albeit in a somewhat adapted form. The cradle songs are particularly beautiful. Shepherds, woodcutters and farm labourers have their own special tunes.

There are no Corsican dance tunes, and no traditional Corsican dances. This fact owes much to the island's unhappy past, which is reflected in their *ballate, lamenti* and *voceri* — improvised laments which they traditionally sing at funerals. These are hardly ever performed these days, and will soon be a thing of the past. The *voceri* in particular were used to set a vendetta in motion. These funeral laments always used to be sung by women. But men sing them now, thus breaking the ancient, time-honoured tradition.

Traditional water fountain at Piana

The art of singing in *paghiella* has been kept in its traditional form. This is an ancient technique in which three tenor voices imitate a lead singer to produce an unusual form of polyphony. There are two places where church mass is still sung in *paghiella* on religious festivals: Sermano near Corte and Rusio in

Castagniccia.

The little that remains of the Corsican traditional costume is worn on special occasions. The women wear a long, spreading dress with black stripes and a black or white-spotted *mandile* — a shoulder or head covering similar to the Spanish *mantilla*. The men wear a wide-brimmed hat and a red sash that was once used for carrying weapons. The colourful clothes that one sees at folk festivals owe more to fantasy than to actual tradition. Black was the traditional colour, since the ongoing vendettas meant that people were usually in mourning.

The only traditional customs are bound up with religious festivals. The most important of these are the Good Friday Procession of the *Catenacciu* at Sartène, and the Festival of the Mother of God at Lavasina near Bastia — the Corsican equivalent of Lourdes, to which pilgrims come from all over the island on 18 May. The Corsicans retain traditional Catholic liturgies that have long since been superseded elsewhere.

The Corsican towns and villages are worthy of special consideration. The people preferred to build them in the mountains, where they were better protected from sea attack. But they depended on the sea for their food, so the fishermen at least had to live on the coast, where they usually built a small harbour — *marina*, or in French *marine*. This state of affairs is still reflected in many of the place names. On Cap Corse, for example, there is Méria on the hillside above the coast and Marine de Méria down below on the shore. The ports are often guarded by fortresses, which were built by various conquering powers to protect them from further invasions.

The towns and villages seem at first sight rather old and dilapidated, with a number of derelict dwellings abandoned by families who have left the island. But on further acquaintance there is a strong sense of romance about them. They are usually built on rock, and the narrow streets are decorated with pots and window boxes full of brightly coloured flowers. The windows themselves are small and heavily shuttered to keep out the heat, and the upper storeys are reached via steep flights of steps.

The hardness of the ground and the lack of drainage meant that special outside pipes had to be laid from the kitchen. These were often nicely decorated. For the same reason, when the toilet was added on later, it was often housed in a little hut on the balcony. Both these features are fast disappearing since the advent of internal piping, though some houses still retain the original decorations where the old pipes used to be.

The big towns and tourist centres have their usual quota of modern shops, flats and hotels, which differ little from their counterparts all over the world. The product of Corsica's recent economic revival, they provide a good basis with which to compare the old traditional Corsican towns.

5. The History of Corsica

There have been people on Corsica since prehistoric times, when dates can only be worked out by scientific means. The oldest known human skeleton on the island goes back to the same period as the earliest known pottery finds. These have been dated back to the Mesolithic period or Middle Stone Age, 8,000 years ago. Some more recent discoveries, however, could possibly go back a further two or three millennia.

Some of the buildings and monoliths from the second and third millennia BC are indicative of more advanced civilisations. But the people that built them disappeared in about 800 BC.

In the meantime the Mediterranean had become a great seafaring region, with the associated spread of power and enlightenment, and especially of trade. But Corsica appears to have remained aloof from this, with little historical or arch-aeological evidence of any kind from this period.

In the twelfth century BC the Phoenicians had begun to sail out from their homeland in present-day Lebanon. They first conquered Crete, thus becoming the first Mediterranean sea power. In the ninth century BC they founded the colony of Carthage, which in turn became the main trading power in the western Mediterranean.

However, the first settlers on Corsica were Greeks from Phocaea on the coast of Asia Minor. In 564 BC they founded the colony of Alalia (now Aléria) on the east coast of the island, which they called Calliste or 'the most beautiful one'.

In 540 BC, in a decisive battle at Alalia, the Greeks were beaten by an alliance of the Carthaginians and Etruscans, which limited their expansion in the western Mediterranean. The Carthaginians took over the colony and called the island Kyrnos, which means 'full of forests'. But in spite of this and the later military domination by Carthage (278–259 BC), the Greeks still

Church with separate bell-tower — legacies of the past

continued to exercise power in the colony, controlling the trade in wood, resin and honey.

The so-called Carthaginian empire was not an empire in the strict sense, since it did not form a single political unit. But it was nonetheless a force to be reckoned with, and this was fully recognised by the next power to come onto the Mediterranean scene — the Romans. They at first allied themselves with Carthage in order to gain ascendancy over the Greeks in southern Italy. But when both powers laid claim to Sicily, this led to a military conflict that was to last more than a century: the three Punic Wars. (The word Punic is derived from *Puni* or *Poeni*, the Latin name for the Phoenicians from whom the Carthaginians were descended.)

Soon after the beginning of the first Punic War (264–241 BC), the Romans took Alalia (259 BC) and began their conquest of Corsica. In 238 BC the Carthaginians officially renounced their claim to the island, which together with Sardinia became the second Roman province (after Sicily). The Romans officially completed their conquest in 163 BC. They called the island Corsica — a corruption of the Carthaginian name Kyrnos. But the inhabitants, who were said to consist of twelve tribes living peaceably together, continued to hold sway in the mountains.

This was why the Romans built their roads along the coasts, although a road is known to have been laid through the Spelunca Gorge. They founded ports and settlements, such as Mariana in 93 BC. Corsica was granted its own senate, which later sent its own representative to the emperor in Rome. In 81 BC Alalia was rebuilt as the port of Aléria, which was to flourish for 500 years. From the second century AD, Christianity began to gain a foothold on the coast. According to legend, the apostle Paul is supposed to have preached on Cap Corse.

In AD 396 the Roman Empire was split in two. Around AD 450 the Vandals came over from North Africa, destroyed Aléria and took over Corsica. After the fall of the Western Empire in AD 476, the Ostrogoths came to the island for a while. Then in AD 552 Corsica became an Eastern Roman province when it was taken over by the Emperor Justinian in his bid to rebuild the Roman Empire.

In 568 the Lombards began to invade Italy from the north. They gradually advanced southwards, and in 725 they took over Corsica. However, their desire to unite Italy did not meet with the approval of the Papacy, and in 754 the Pope turned to France for assistance. Pepin the Short of France engaged in a successful campaign against the Lombards, and in 756 handed over some of the territory he had gained to the Pope. Known as Pepin's Gift, it later formed the basis for the development of the Papal States. Corsica was part of this gift, but was one of the territories whose administration the Pope left to others. So the Corsicans were at the mercy of whatever governor happened to be in charge.

In the meantime the Arabs, united and spurred on by the teachings of Mohammed, had begun to conquer the Mediterranean. In those days they were known as the Saracens. For 200 years, Corsica lay in the midst of their sea routes, and was repeatedly subjected to attacks and invasions. During the periods in between, the island was tyrannised by a series of

Pisan lookout tower, Porto

power-crazed nobles who caused the islanders to flee into the mountains.

In 1077 the Pope eventually handed over Corsica to the Bishop of Pisa, and the island enjoyed a short period of relative peace. The Pisans are said to have ruled Corsica wisely, justly and charitably, showing genuine concern for the welfare of its long-suffering inhabitants. They also took care of the Corsicans' spiritual welfare, and are supposed to have founded 300 Christian churches on the island, removing the last remaining traces of paganism.

This aroused the envy of the nearby city republic of Genoa, which had a flourishing sea trade in the region. The Pope eventually gave in to pressure, and in 1138 divided the island between Pisa and Genoa. But the Genoese were not satisfied with just the northern half of the island. They took over Bonifacio in 1195, and Calvi in 1278; in 1284 they routed the Pisan fleet, and in 1299 the Pisans gave up the island.

The people of Corsica had been divided by these struggles, and had sometimes been called upon to fight one another during a difficult period that gave no promise of improvement. This was the time of the great Corsican hero Sinucello della Rocca, whose name went down in history as the first of the great Corsican freedom-fighters.

However, as soon as the Pisans had withdrawn, another rival power appeared. For in 1297 the Pope had handed over the territories of Corsica and Sardinia to the kingdom of Aragon in Spain. In the struggle for supremacy, the Corsican nobility supported Aragon, while the people now sided with Genoa. In 1420 King Alfonso V of Aragon staged a military invasion, but 14 years later his Corsican viceroy was captured and executed by the Genoese.

Less than twenty years later, in 1451, Christopher Columbus was born, though it is not known for certain whether he was Corsican as the islanders claim. He is known to have given his nationality as Genoese, but this does not rule out Corsica, since he could have been forced to say this for political reasons. The actual truth will probably never be known.

The power of the Genoese was dependent on the financial backing of a group of merchants who in 1408 had founded an important bank. In 1453 they took over the administration of Corsica. They showed no mercy in putting down local rebellions, but failed to bring about peace.

A 100 years later Sampiero Corso, a Corsican officer in the French army, attempted to improve the lot of his homeland by bringing it under French sovereignty. The result of this was 3 years of war, followed by 3 years of French rule, 5 years of Genoese rule and a further 3 years of war. At the end of this the Genoese remained the sole rulers. Many Corsicans left the island in despair. Some of them went to Rome to serve the Pope, where they became the famous Corsican Guard.

The eighteenth century was another period of great troubles. They began in 1729, when the Corsicans rebelled against the oppressive rule of the Genoese, whose power was now waning. In 1736 the Corsicans declared themselves an independent kingdom. At the same time a German adventurer called Baron von Neuhoff landed with a small troop at Aléria and promised to rescue them from Genoese tyranny. They made him king for a few months, but soon came to realise that what he had promised was no more than bluff. He also showed no understanding of Corsican customs, immediately declaring the vendetta to be punishable by death. It was soon obvious that the promised reinforcements from abroad were mere fantasy, and he was forced to flee the island under cover of darkness.

The Corsican coat of arms has been attributed by some to Baron von Neuhoff. It consists of a Moor's head wearing a white headband. The headband was supposed to be a symbol of slavery since most slaves were Moors. It was said that von Neuhoff had once jumped into the sea to rescue a slave from drowning. But in actual fact the coat of arms goes back to the crusades. The Moors, who fought against the crusaders, used the headband as a symbol of royal dignity, and flew this coat of arms on all their royal ships. It became a favourite trophy for the Corsicans when they fought against the Moors, whom they generally assumed to be Saracen infidels — and they eventually adopted it for themselves. The Genoese adapted the Corsican flag as a way of exerting their power over them. They turned the headband into a blindfold by placing it over the eyes. But from the time of Pasquale Paoli the royal headband was returned to its original position.

Pasquale Paoli was proclaimed General of the Corsican Nation in 1755. He was the greatest of a long line of Corsican heroes during their long struggle for freedom. He made Corte his capital and declared this newly independent state a constitutional democracy. In this he was a long way ahead of his time, and with his programme of economic and social recovery he gave hope and inspiration to his people.

European rulers such as Frederic the Great of Germany and Katherine of Russia looked on in amazement at the developments on this island. Jean-Jacques Rousseau, on whose theories the constitution was based, offered his admiring support. Paoli worked hard towards his ultimate goal, building a new port at Ile Rousse because Calvi and Bastia were still under Genoese

Les Calanches cliffs

Typical Corsican beach

Ota

L'Ile Rousse

Statue of Pasquale Paoli, Corte

domination. In 1764, he even founded a university at Corte, which sadly lasted only 25 years.

The blow came in 1768, when the news came that Genoa had effectively sold Corsica to the French. Paoli pursued all possible diplomatic channels in his efforts to retain Corsica's hard-won independence, but to no avail. The French brought in their troops, who defeated Paoli's army at Ponte Nuovo on 9 May 1769. The Corsicans had been forced down to the bottom of the valley, and had not been able to attack from above as was their wont. Paoli himself fled to England. On 15 August that year, Napoléon Bonaparte was born in Ajaccio, the son of a Corsican notary.

About twenty years later Paoli was pardoned by Louis XVI, and returned to his native island. In 1791 he was made governor of Corsica, but soon came into conflict with the French revolutionary authorities. He immediately convened his old Corsican parliament, which declared the island independent for a second time, requesting the British to provide military support. Admiral Hood came along and took both Calvi and Bastia. Horatio Nelson, who was later to become the great British admiral, lost his eye in this campaign as a result of a shot from a Corsican gun.

In 1794 Corsica was declared an apanage of the British crown, but the situation lasted no more than 2 years. For the Corsicans were bitterly disappointed at not being granted full independence, and were angry when the British placed a viceroy over them. Under pressure both from the Corsicans and from the French army in Italy, Britain renounced its claim to the island. Ironically, the French army was under the command of a Corsican general called Napoléon Bonaparte, who in 1793 had held on to Bonifacio for France.

By this time the Corsicans had resigned themselves to French rule, realising that they were unable to retain their independence, and having decided that the French were the lesser of the two evils. In 1795 their great hero Pasquale Paoli, who was by now almost 70 years old, returned to England, where he died in 1807. Since that time the history of Corsica has been bound up with that of France.

General Napoléon Bonaparte was later to become Emperor Napoléon I of France, thus becoming the greatest Corsican of them all. It cannot, however, be said that he did anything to further Corsica's freedom as all its previous heroes had done.

In World War II the Corsicans came under occupation again. It was only for a short time from 1942-3, but it was enough to rekindle the old spirit of freedom. They gave enthusiastic support to the French resistance movement under General de Gaulle, so that the German and Italian occupying forces were soon compelled to leave the island.

6. Art and Culture

The beginnings of art and culture go back to earliest times, when people started to make their own tools and to think about life and death. The early hunter-gatherers might well have simply lived for each day, but they probably made observations about the world around them that led them to reflect, to experiment and eventually to develop techniques for growing crops and breeding livestock.

Before people learned to use metal, they discovered how to work clay. It was easier to work into the desired shape than stone, bone or wood by carving, and it was more durable than any woven or matted material.

The seasonal nature of farming would have provided people with leisure time to specialise. There was time to think more deeply and creatively about the tools and artefacts that they made. There was also a chance to make less functional objects that were beautiful to look at and reflected the sensibilities of their creator. The result of all this might be termed a work of art — the product of both skill and creative thought.

The first art, however, goes back to the time of the early hunters, when a successful hunt must have caused them to believe in luck. They must have tried to bring about more luck by making drawings of the animals they hunted. Only gradually would they have noticed a pattern that was more ordered than luck, and which must therefore be subject to some higher power.

It may even be that the proverb 'Man proposes, God disposes' goes back to a concept that was already understood in those early times. People must have personalised this ever-present natural order in the form of a god, whom they attempted to approach and understand, and even to influence.

Moreover, people were earthbound as long as they lived — but what happened after death? Was it possible to live on beyond death, or even to be born into a new life? Such questions must have been asked in those times. People most probably answered them by turning to a god whom they felt they could trust for eternity.

In order to represent this god, they would naturally have used stone, which was the most lasting and permanent material they had. They used it to build the altars on which they made sacrifices to their god. And then they built stone temples — earthly dwellings for their god, where he might be present at the ceremonies that they performed on his behalf. These temples

Carved standing stones, Filitosa

would also have provided them with a refuge from the great unknown — that power which they could sense but could not comprehend, and that filled them with awe and fear.

Their desire to live on after death found expression in the ways that they buried their dead, first in holes in the rock, then in stone coffins and tombs, which they decorated with gravestones and monuments. These stone memorials have lasted to this day, just as their creators intended — and apart from ornaments and tools they are the chief evidence that today's archaeologists can use in order to make sense of the cultures that created them.

There is evidence in Corsica of two ancient cultures that venerated the dead in this way. One of these is mostly represented by the menhirs and dolmens of the Neolithic period (New Stone Age), the other in the camps and tombs of the Bronze Age that followed it.

The remains of the Megalithic culture of the New Stone Age are mostly to be found in the south-west of the island. The fact that there are no sites further north could reflect the settlement patterns as much as the religious beliefs of the indigenous population.

The Megalithic culture appears to have covered the whole of Europe and western Asia, and the discoveries in the western Mediterranean are in many ways remarkably alike. But the findings on Corsica — the menhirs in particular — reveal some peculiarities of their own. They consist of upright stones, usually between 1m and 2m high (though sometimes as high as 4m), and the later ones are carved in the form of human faces and bodies. These are described in stories and legends as eternal bodies in which the souls of the dead live on. Archaeologists call them menhir statues or statue stones.

They developed in three phases, the first of which started in about 3000 BC. The menhirs from this period were between 1m and 2m high, were hardly carved at all, and were simply placed on top of the graves. Each grave was made up of a stone coffin placed in the ground, which was covered with earth or a series of carefully prepared layers of stones. Standing stones were then placed in a single or double circle around the grave mound. Mass graves have also been found in this form. Sometimes the menhir was placed directly in the coffin, from which it stuck up out of the ground.

In the second phase, around 2000 BC, the menhirs were often larger (up to 4m high), and revealed the first attempts at real sculpture. They were often as far as 30m away from the tombs themselves, which were now built above ground in the form of dolmens. The menhirs were placed in a long row, or sometimes in a set of two or three parallel rows, known as an alignment. The rows ran in a north-south direction, with the menhirs facing east towards the rising sun.

The third phase began in about 1500 BC, by which time the menhirs were being carved into true statues as the Megalithic culture reached its peak. They were now often no longer in the vicinity of a grave, but simply near a mound with an altar. This would suggest that by this time the menhirs were not actually associated with one dead person in particular, but were simply

One of Corsica's many magnificent dolmens

part of the religious cult of the period.

These menhir statues display yet another, rather puzzling feature: the figures carry weapons — swords and daggers that were entirely foreign to the Megalithic culture. They were, however, already present in the Bronze Age cultures of the Aegean. Why, then, should these Stone Age Corsicans have depicted something that was foreign to their culture?

The answer to this question lies in an area to the south-east of the island, where archaeologists have discovered the very weapons that the Megalithic statues depicted. These were found on the sites of a new and different culture that built massive structures made up of layers of gigantic stones. The ceilings were vaulted using a technique known as false vaulting or corbel vaulting. But the most striking features of these sites are the round, tower-like structures that stand overlooking them, and after which this new civilisation was named — Torreans, from *torre*, the Italian for tower. There is no doubt that they were immigrants to Corsica, since they have left no traces from before 2000 BC.

These people seem to have lived quietly and peacefully near a sheltered bay in the south-east of Corsica. They were probably a seafaring race that took more interest in lands across the sea than in the hinterland behind them.

But from about 1500 BC they began to move inland and inevitably came into conflict with the indigenous Megalithic culture. The result was that both peoples began to build defensive fortresses. It is in this context that the weapons carried by the figures in the late Megalithic statues can be fully understood as the trappings of an alien culture.

It was not that the Megalithic people wished to do homage to these newcomers. Rather, they may have hoped that by making stone effigies of them they might somehow keep them at a distance. That they were convinced of the efficacy of these statues is borne out by the carefully thought-out craftsmanship that they reveal. For they represent Megalithic sculpture at its most advanced. There is no evidence that the arrival of these new neighbours created any instability in their society, which appears to have made a positive adjustment to the new situation.

Close examination of these Megalithic representations of Torrean warriors reveals a number of interesting features. They wore belts round their waists for carrying their swords, rib-like breastplates and horned helmets. All of these features were familiar to archaeologists, who had seen them on wall frescos at the temple of Medinet-Habu near Luxor in Egypt. Now these were supposed to be Shardans — a seafaring race that were to be found all over the Mediterranean region. It has not yet been proved that the Torreans were in actual fact Shardans, let alone that they were forerunners of the Vikings, as certain Scandinavian researchers would claim!

But whatever the case, it is certain that by 1400 BC the Torreans had advanced right into the Megalithic heartlands around Filitosa. The hill on which the main Megalithic temple was built was then turned into a Torrean fortress. What is more, the Torreans, as if to emphasise their victory and their contempt for the Megalithic cult, smashed the menhirs to pieces and used them for building stone.

Archaeologists have uncovered a large number of these remnants of menhirs during their investigations of the Torrean tower temples. The juxtaposition of these two civilisations makes Filitosa the most interesting archaeological site on Corsica.

Then both cultures disappeared from southern Corsica. The Megalithics moved further north, where a number of menhirs

Pisan architecture — St Michael's Church, Murato

remain, though they no longer represented warriors. The Torreans left Filitosa in about 1200 BC, and appear to have gone south to Sardinia, where the tower temples known as the *Nuraghi* are thought by some to be derived from the *Torri* of Corsica.

There is a gap in the archaeological record from about 800 BC until the time of the Romans. There are relatively few Roman remains, the main sites being at **Aléria** and at **Mariana** just south of Bastia Airport. There is nothing that is distinctively Corsican about anything that remains from this period.

Following the period of Roman occupation, Corsica became part of the Byzantine Empire. During the dark ages there were a number of Benedictine monasteries on the island, which are supposed to have exerted a strong cultural and religious influence. However, there are no surviving traces of them left on Corsica.

The defensive ramparts of Bonifacio

The oldest surviving religious building is the Romanesque chapel of St Mary at **Quenza** near Zonza, where a stone next to the side door is inscribed with the date AD 1000. Soon after this date, the Pisans took over the island, and built many more churches in the Romanesque style of architecture, popular in Tuscany, which was influenced by Lombardy and Byzantium. Several of these churches have survived to the present day.

The finest example from this period is St Michael's Church near **Murato** — a rectangular structure built of blue and white stones in a mosaic pattern. The bell tower is partly supported on two columns so that it overhangs the main entrance — a unique feature that cannot even be found in Italy. Another famous Pisan church is Ste Marie de Nebbio near **St Florent**, where the bishop is supposed to have kept a pistol by the altar during mass. It has the same ground plan as the famous church known as La Canonica at **Mariana**, which, although founded in 1120, was destroyed in the sixteenth century and rebuilt in the twentieth. The church of St Christine at **Cervione** contains another Pisan feature that is found only on Corsica — the twin apse.

The Pisans also had to protect the island against invaders, but the only remaining Pisan defences are a few ruined lookout towers on the coast such as the one near Porto (see page 45).

They are rectangular, as opposed to the round Genoese towers such as the Tour de la Parata (see page 82).

The Genoese also built citadels to guard all the towns, and these are still very much part of the typical Corsican scene. They were built during the fifteenth and sixteenth centuries in the typically functional style of the period. The Genoese bridges, of which several still remain, were similarly functional in style. They consist mostly of only one arch, such as the one near Albertacce in Niolo. The most famous, however, is the old five-arched bridge of **Ponte Nuovo** (see page 75), of which the two middle arches have fallen into the river. The monasteries of the time were also fortified, but nearly all of them have fallen into ruin since the time of the French Revolution.

As regards church architecture, the Romanesque style was followed by the Gothic, of which the only examples on Corsica are parts of certain churches in **Bonifacio** such as St Dominic's and Ste Marie Majeure. The one example of Renaissance architecture is St Antony's Oratory at **Calvi**.

Most of the present-day churches were built between the sixteenth and eighteenth centuries, and are predominantly Baroque in style. But there are very few pure examples, as they were often built over a long period of time. The best, however, is probably St Mary's at **Bastia**. The Imperial Chapel in **Ajaccio** is an example of the neoclassical style. It was built by Napoléon III as a memorial to Napoléon I.

The best art is to be found in the churches and chapels, which are often quite beautifully decorated. The best-preserved of the few surviving medieval frescos are in the old Pisan church of St Michael near **Murato** (see above). The Genoese used rather more decoration in their churches. There are beautiful altars combining different kinds of marble, elaborate fonts and impressive reliefs. Many of these treasures were crafted in Genoa and shipped across to Corsica. The finest statues on the island are in the monastery at **Alesani**. The Musée Fesch in Ajaccio houses a collection of Italian paintings from the four-teenth to the eighteenth centuries.

Wood carvings are the only handicrafts that are native to Corsica; they reflect clearly the long and bitter struggles of its people. The saints are usually portrayed as crusaders riding into battle; the madonnas have an air of severity, suffering and determination, while representations of Christ on the cross are particularly moving and expressive.

1 THE NORTHERN WEST COAST

Ajaccio • Cargèse • Porto • Calvi (163km)

The D81 forms the main coast road from Ajaccio to Calvi. It branches off the main N195 Corte and Bastia road at **Mezzavia**, just outside **Ajaccio**. It climbs over several mountain passes, and sometimes follows the irregularities of the coastline, but there are some fairly fast sections as well.

The first section (52km) goes from Ajaccio to Cargèse at the northern end of the Gulf of Sagone. It first crosses the mountain ridges that run to the north of Ajaccio. Only 20km out of the town, it reaches the top of the **Col de San Bastiano** (410m), where there is a marvellous view of the coast to the north, with the ever-present mountains in the background.

The road joins the coast, and runs past a number of old lookout towers — just a few of the many such towers that pepper the Corsican coastline. Sandy beaches alternate with rocky headlands, and the small villages thrive on the trade that tourism brings.

The largest of these is **Sagone**, which is 38km from Ajaccio. It has a lovely wide beach, which provides ideal conditions for sailing and windsurfing. The small harbour exports agricultural products from the neighbouring region of Cinarca. Sagone was originally founded by the Romans, and was later a port and cathedral town. There are very few remains of the old twelfth-century cathedral, which was built round the old apse of a fourth-century church.

There is a turning at Sagone along the D70, which runs through the beautiful scenery of **Cinarca** to **Vico** (13km) and the **Forêt d'Aitone** .

The D81 continues along the coast, and soon comes within sight of **Cargèse**. This small town is situated on the headland that forms the northern boundary of the Gulf of Sagone. It clings to the hillside, 60-80m above the waters of the bay. It was founded in 1774 by Greeks who had settled on Corsica a century earlier. A modern memorial on the cliff top reminds us of this fact.

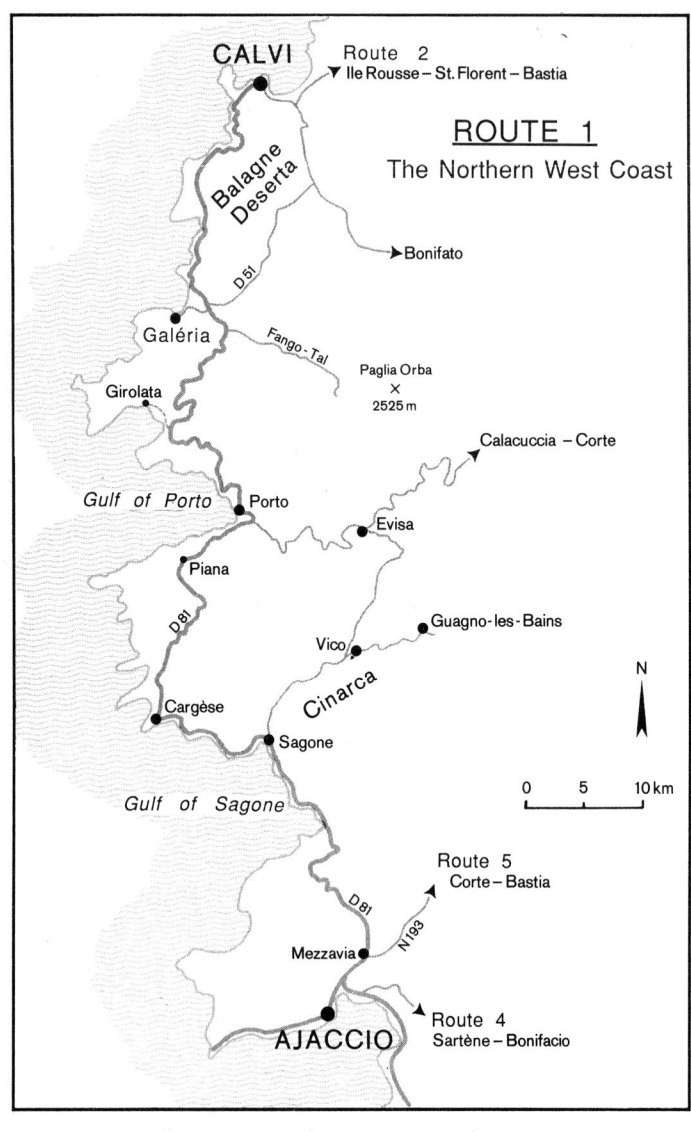

CALVI

Route 2
Ile Rousse – St. Florent – Bastia

ROUTE 1

The Northern West Coast

Balagne
Deserta

D 51

Bonifato

Galéria

Fango-Tal

Paglia Orba
×
2525 m

Girolata

Calacuccia – Corte

Gulf of Porto   Porto

Evisa

Piana

D 81

Guagno-les-Bains

Vico

Cinarca

Cargèse

Sagone

N

Gulf of Sagone

0   5   10 km

Route 5
Corte – Bastia

D 81

Mezzavia

N 193

Route 4
Sartène – Bonifacio

AJACCIO

The Greeks nowadays speak mostly French and Corsican, and have adopted the Corsican way of life; but they still adhere closely to their Orthodox faith. The Roman Catholic and Greek Orthodox churches stand opposite one another on two hills separated by a hollow. The Orthodox church contains some beautiful icons of saints. There are special ceremonies in Holy Week, especially on Good Friday evening, when the people sing haunting Greek dirges in the darkening shadows of the unlit church.

The most popular beach in the vicinity is the Plage de Pero, which is situated along the next small bay to the north.

The road leaves the coast for the next 20km from Cargèse to **Piana**. There is a view of the sea from the **Col de Terracia** (100m). Then the road runs along a river valley with heavily cultivated terraced slopes. It climbs steeply again, and shortly before Piana it reaches the top of the **Col de Lava** (498m). The pass provides a magnificent view of the **Gulf of Porto**, which is considered by some to be the most beautiful bay on the island.

Piana is a marvellous resort for holidaymakers who prefer to stay away from the beach. It is situated 438m above the shore, and there are lots of walks through the neighbouring woodlands and *maquis* (see page 91).

12km beyond Piana, the road runs for 2km along **Les Calanches** (in French, Calanques), which form Corsica's most amazing natural phenomenon. These yellowish-red cliffs plunge vertically into the sea from a height of 200-300m, and have been eroded into the most bizarre and fascinating shapes. Coaches often stop so that passengers can walk a short way on foot.

The road winds down the hillside to the Porto estuary, where an old Pisan lookout tower stands on a headland above the bay, and a grove of eucalyptus trees runs along the beach of **Marine de Porto**. A small port handles the shipment of chestnuts, olives and wood from the hinterland, and offers boat trips to the grottos along the bay and up the coast to Girolata (see below).

The road crosses the river about 2km inland. Just before the bridge there is a turning along the D84 for Evisa , which continues via Corsica's highest pass into the beautiful region of Niolo .

The small town of **Porto** lies on the north bank of the river. Porto is a popular holiday resort, and is no longer inhabited exclusively by artists, though they still come here to try and capture the beauty of the rocky bay and the forests on their sketchpads and canvases. The nearby beaches of Serriera and

Porto — a popular holiday resort

Partinello remain closed to tourists.

Porto is exactly half-way between Ajaccio and Calvi, being about 80km from both. The D81 continues northwards from Porto, partly along the hillside overlooking the Gulf of Porto. There are marvellous views of the beaches below, and of the bizarre cliffs on the south side of the bay. The road twists and climbs over the **Col de la Croix** (272m), which provides a final view of the Gulf of Porto. A side-road leads down to the Plage de Gratelle.

Ahead to the left is the **Gulf of Girolata** — yet another of the wonders of Corsica, with boat trips from Marine de Porto (see above) and even from Calvi. There is no road to it as yet, although one is planned very soon. At present it is an hour's journey on foot to the small fishing village of **Girolata**, which provides facilities for yachtsmen and divers. Nearby are the ruins of a Genoese fort.

The road winds downhill and then climbs steeply again. After 11km it reaches the top of the **Col de Palmarella** (374m). There is a final glimpse of the Gulf of Girolata, and a fine view ahead of a region of forests surrounded by peaks of 800-900m. The road descends sharply, and after a further 11km it arrives at a river called the Fango.

There is a right turn along a side road, which goes 13½km

The Gulf of Balagne

along the beautiful **Fango Valley** to Bardiana. There are impressive views of the massive **Capo Tafonato** (2,343m), which is easily recognisable from the great hole in the side of its peak. According to legend, the hole is quite literally the work of the devil, who, angry at seeing St Martin farming peacefully among the highlands of Balagne, is supposed to have hit the peak with his club. To the left of Capo Tafonato is the majestic **Paglia Orba** (2,525m), the most beautiful mountain in Corsica.

2km further along the main road, there is a left turn along a side road to the small coastal resort of **Galéria** (4km), which is situated in a rocky bay with nice sandy beaches. The small harbour is used to export charcoal.

The road to Calvi crosses the Fango via a long concrete bridge. Immediately after that, the D51 goes off to the right, forming the more direct route to Calvi through the mountains. But visitors are recommended to continue along the D81 coast road. Although longer (30km) and much more twisty, it goes along a particularly fine stretch of coastline. It mounts a ridge called **Bocca Bassa** (122m), from which there is a lovely view of Galéria and the mountains behind.

The road enters the **Balagne Deserta**, which stretches from here as far as Calvi. Its name is misleading, for although drier than the fertile Balagne proper to the east of Calvi, it is a wilderness rather than a desert, and forms a region of *maquis*-covered hills.

 About half-way to Calvi, the road passes the Tour Mozza on the right. Originally an old lookout tower, it was converted into a residence by Napoléon's pleasure-seeking nephew Pierre. Further along to the left, and down towards the coast, is another tower called the Tour Truccia. The lighthouse on **Cap Cavallo** is clearly visible ahead.

The road continues close to the irregular coastline. About 5km before Calvi, it crosses the **Revellata Peninsula**. There is a right turn along a side-road to the church of Madonna della Serra, which stands on a rocky outcrop overlooking Calvi.

The ancient Genoese fortress town of **Calvi** is situated on a high, rocky promontory that juts out into the sea, affording a marvellous view of the mountains inland and of the coastline which follows.

2 THE NORTH COAST

Calvi • Ile Rousse • St Florent • Bastia (93km)

It is less than 100km from Calvi to Bastia, but there are many possible detours on the way that have much to recommend them. Near the start of the route there are detours through Balagne (see page 131), which add no more than 18km to the distance. Nearer to Bastia, one can make detours either through Nebbio, adding an extra 17km, or around the coast of Cap Corse, adding at least 85km to the distance. Alternatively, one can make special excursions to these regions from bases at Calvi or Ile Rousse on the one hand, or at Bastia or St Florent on the other.

The main route goes along the N197 from **Calvi** to Ile Rousse. 3km out of Calvi, there is a right turn for St Cathérine's International Airport and Bonifato. Another 1km further on is another right turn for Calenzana in Balagne. The road then begins to climb as it crosses one of the spurs of the Cinto massif. There is a view back across the bay to Calvi.

5km further on is the village of **Lumio**, which clings precariously to the hillside above the road. Just after Lumio, there is a right turn along the D71, which forms the main road through **Balagne**. It winds and twists for 32km through glorious scenery until it arrives at Belgodère. One can then either turn left to return to the north coast (8km), or turn right for Ponte Leccia (33km) on the Ajaccio-Bastia road (see route 5). For a much shorter detour, one can turn left off the D71 at Cateri and go via Corbara to Ile Rousse.

The main route returns to the coast. After barely 3km, there is a view of the small coastal resort of **Marine de Sant' Ambroggio.** 2km further on is **Algajola**, which is crowned by the restored remains of a massive seventeenth-century fortress. The church contains a few interesting paintings. The nearby quarry provided the building stone for Napoléon's tomb in Les Invalides in Paris.

The road carries on over the **Col de Carbonal** (88m). On the shore below is another recently developed holiday resort called

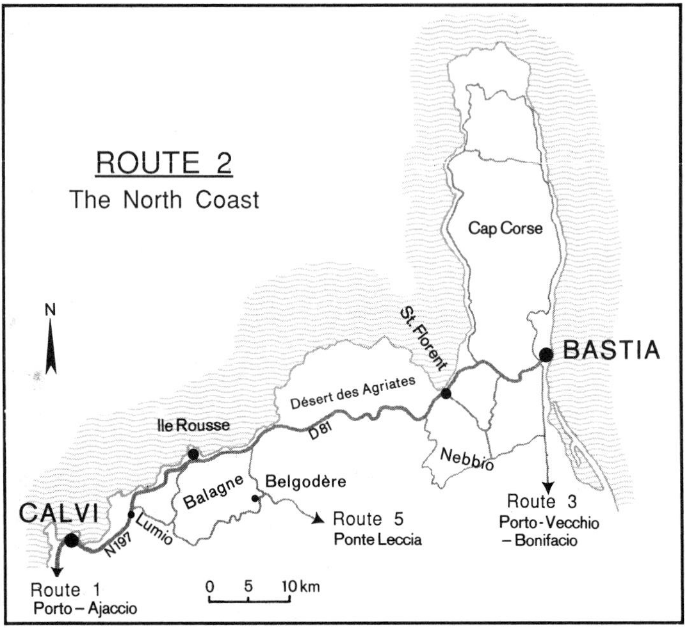

ROUTE 2
The North Coast

N

Cap Corse

BASTIA

St. Florent

Désert des Agriates

Ile Rousse

D81

Nebbio

Balagne   Belgodère

CALVI   Lumio

N197

Route 5
Ponte Leccia

Route 3
Porto-Vecchio
– Bonifacio

Route 1
Porto – Ajaccio

0   5   10 km

Marine de Davia. The rocky coast here forms a number of small sandy bays. On the approach to Ile Rousse the road crosses the **Col de Folgato**, from which there are views of the coast in both directions. At this point the road comes in from Balagne via Corbara (see above).

Ile Rousse (population 2,500) is built on the site of an old Roman settlement. It rivals Calvi as a seaside resort, having wide, sandy beaches, a casino and good accommodation facilities. There is a historical basis to this rivalry. For the port of Ile Rousse was built by Pasquale Paoli in 1758 to replace Calvi, which was still in the hands of the Genoese. It has now overtaken Calvi as a port, exporting fresh fruit and olive oil from Balagne.

The harbour is situated on an island, which is reached via a bridge. The island is no more than a massive, reddish-coloured rock that juts out into the sea — hence the name Ile Rousse, which means 'russet island'. There is a lighthouse at the outer end of the island, with an old ruined tower in front and to the left.

Returning to the mainland, one enters the old town along the

Hotel Napoléon Bonaparte, Ile Rousse

Rue Napoléon. This leads to the Place Paoli — a square surrounded by plane trees that forms the centre of the town. In the middle of the square is a bust of Paoli himself. His friends preferred to call the town Paolina. The old market hall is situated on the corner of the Rue Napoléon. The church to the right of the square was built in 1914 in the neoclassical style. To the left is the one-time Palazzo Piccioni, which has since been converted into the Hotel Napoléon Bonaparte.

For those not interested in the beach, Ile Rousse forms an ideal centre for visiting the beautiful region of **Balagne**.

The N197 continues along the cliffs overlooking the shore. After about 7km, the tower on the left affords a magnificent view back to Ile Rousse. The road then turns slightly inland to cross the River Regino. Immediately after that there is a junction: the N197 turns south-east across the mountains to Belgodère and Ponte Leccia, but the present route turns left along the D81 for St Florent and Bastia.

To the left is a good sandy beach with tourist facilities. The D81 leaves the broad, fertile valley and climbs up onto the cliffs again. It passes **Cima Arca** (319m) to the left, which is the site of some interesting dolmen remains. There are views back along the coast to Ile Rousse, and small stony beaches can occasionally be glimpsed down on the shore.

The road comes to a bay with a wide beach and sand dunes. At this point the coast turns sharply northwards, while the road continues due east, passing to the south of a barren coastal region called the **Désert des Agriates**. This impenetrable wilderness stretches for 30km as far as St Florent. It is hilly and covered in *maquis*, and has a wild beauty all of its own.

The road descends briefly to cross the Ostriconi, then climbs along the side of the Termine Valley to the **Col de Lavezzo** (312m), which is 11km from the sea. There is a magnificent view inland across the mountains as far as Monte Cinto itself. One can also look east past the pyramid-shaped Monte Genova (418m) to the Gulf of St Florent and Cap Corse. The views are even better from Monte Lavezzo (412m), which requires a half-hour climb on foot. From here one can see back along the coast as far as Ile Rousse.

About a mile further on the road crosses a four-arched bridge called the Pont du Diable, which means 'devil's bridge'. The road continues to twist and turn through the hills. The only proper village it passes is **Casta**, 12km before St Florent. Eventually the road begins to descend towards the Gulf of St Florent, which again is one of the most beautiful bays in Corsica.

5km before St Florent there is a left turn for San Pietro-di-Tenda. 4km further on there is another turning along a somewhat better road to Oletta. Both roads afford possible detours through **Nebbio** (see page 113).

The small town of **St Florent** is situated on a small peninsula to the east of the Aliso estuary. It looks pretty when viewed from a distance, and the little that remains of the old town has a decidedly romantic air, in contrast to the modern buildings that surround it.

Napoléon once had great plans for developing the town, but these were never actually realised. The citadel once guarded a bustling port; but the harbour has been allowed to silt up, while the fifteenth-century fortifications have since fallen into ruin. All that remain are the small, brightly-painted fishing and sailing boats that come in on the tide; the big ships are handled at Bastia. The old port headquarters has been turned into the Centre d'Etudes Sous-Marines (Centre for Underwater Studies).

But in recent years St Florent, thanks to its fine sandy beach and its beautiful setting, has found a new role as holiday and watersports centre *par excellence*. It has a well-appointed marina (in French, *port de plaisance*), offering training courses in sailing, diving and windsurfing. For those who wish to explore the hinterland, there is ramblers' centre and even a horseriding association. There are boat trips along the west side of the bay to the Fornali and Mortella lighthouses.

Just outside the town is the fascinating thirteenth-century basilica of **Ste Marie de Nebbio** or Santa Maria dell' Assunta. It was built in the Pisan style out of marble from Táranto. The arch friezes and column capitals are particularly impressive. A side chapel off the south aisle houses the reputed relics of St Florent himself, who served in the Roman army in the third century and was executed as a martyr. Not far away are the remains of the seventeenth-century bishop's palace.

It is only 23km from St Florent to Bastia, taking the direct route across the mountains of **Cap Corse**. A detour around the coast of this long and beautiful peninsula adds a considerable distance to the journey, but has much to recommend it (see page 103).

The road soon leaves the Gulf of St Florent, and after 5km it arrives at the **Col de San Bernardino** (76m), where the Cap Corse coast road turns off. 1km further on towards Bastia is the wine-producing village of **Patrimonio**, which is popular with visitors who wish to sample its wines. The village is laid out in terraces on the side of a hill, which is crowned by a beautiful old church.

Those interested in prehistory are recommended to visit the menhir in the garden of the mayor's residence. The so-called 'Man of Patrimonio' was discovered nearby in 1964. It was found in four pieces, but has since been restored to something like its original

Patrimonio

state. It is 2.29m high, and the head is exceptionally well sculpted, thanks to the softness of the stone. It is only the second limestone menhir to have been found on Corsica.

The nearby village of **Barbaggio** is similarly renowned for its wines. It is a further 7km to the **Col de Teghime** (549m). The road climbs through rich vegetation across slopes covered in vineyards. There is a particularly steep section leading up to the top of the pass. From the top there is a beautiful panorama of the mountains to the south, the Gulf of St Florent behind, and Bastia and the sea to the east ahead. There is a monument to battles which took place here in 1943. More energetic visitors are recommended to climb a further 400m to the nearby peak of **Serra di Pigno**, which is 4km away, and is topped by a radio and TV mast.

The remaining 10km to **Bastia** is through *maquis* and forest, past the monastery of St Antoine and the orchards that cover the lower slopes. Before tackling the final steep section into Corsica's largest town, it is worth stopping to look at the view. To the south is a long coastal lagoon called the Etang de Biguglia. This forms part of the broad floodplain where the next route begins.

3 THE EAST COAST

Bastia • Moriani • Aléria • Porto-Vecchio • Bonifacio (170km)

This route should be considered primarily as a means of getting quickly from north to south, or to the many resorts along the coast. There are 46km to Prunete, a further 97km to Porto-Vecchio, and 27km along the final section to Bonifacio. The total journey can be easily accomplished in 2 hours.

Only two parts of the route are of scenic interest. The first is the 26km section from Casamozza to Prunete, which runs along the foot of the mountains of Casinca and Castagniccia. The second is the 41km section from Solenzara to Porto-Vecchio, which passes close to the Bavella hill-country and the Forêt de l'Ospédale. However, both of these regions warrant a special detour or an excursion to themselves.

The route leaves **Bastia** along the N193 past the old citadel, where there is a good view of the plains to the south. The road crosses these plains in a dead-straight line, and the 20km journey to Casamozza is quickly accomplished.

The road passes close to a number of interesting places. To the left is a lagoon called the **Etang de Biguglia**, which is surrounded by reedbeds, orchards and vineyards. On the tongue of land that divides it from the sea are the first of the many hotels and holiday centres that are springing up next to beaches all the way down the coast.

On the slopes to the right, 5km from Bastia, is the village of **Furiani** (150m), which has the remains of an old Genoese fortress that was captured by the Corsicans in 1729. 3km further on, on a hill to the right, is the village of **Biguglia** (270m), which the Pisans and Genoese used as the capital of Corsica until the founding of Bastia. It affords a commanding view of the plain, the lagoon and the beach.

1km further on is the junction with the D82 St Florent road, which goes through the **Défilé de Lancone** into the region of **Nebbio** (see page 113). Another 7km further, on another hill to the right, is the village of **Borgo** (320m), which is dominated by a

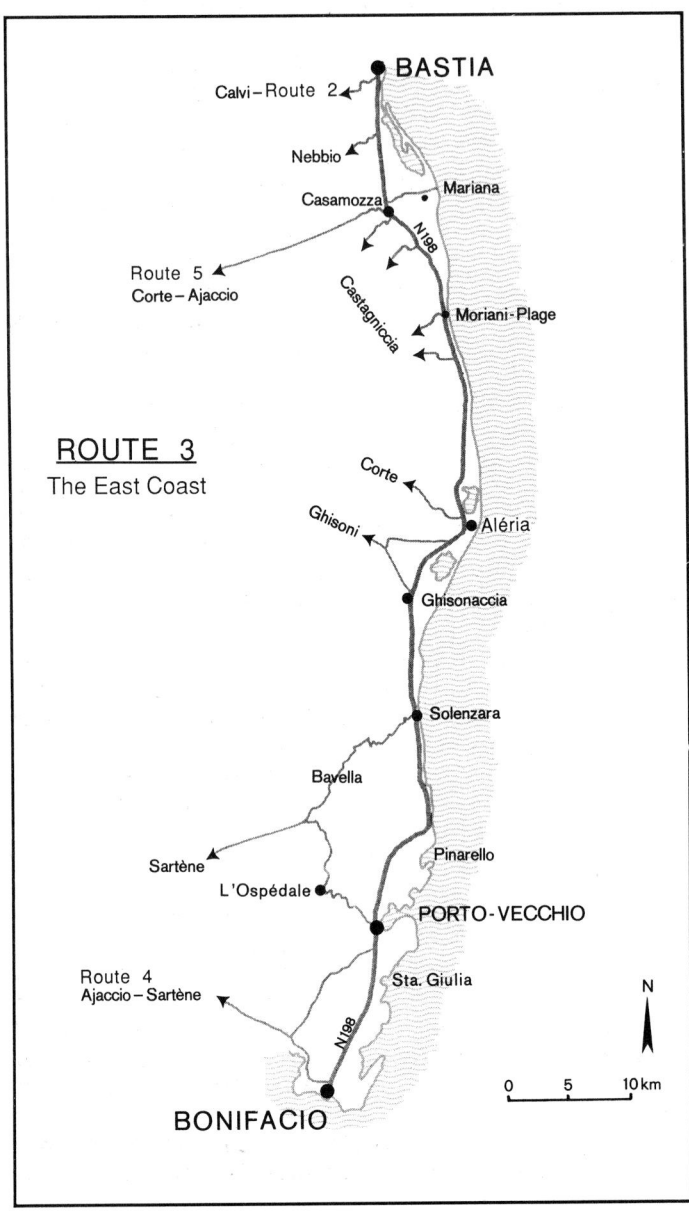

free-standing bell-tower. Pasquale Paoli won a victory here in 1768.

Then there is a turning to the left for **Poretta Airport** (3km), which serves as the airport for Bastia. This was where the French author and pilot Antoine de Saint-Exupéry took off for the last time on 31 July 1944, on a flight from which he never returned. There is a simple monument to his memory.

If one turns right just before the airport and continues for another 5½km, one eventually arrives at the famous St Mary's Basilica, known as La Canonica, which was built in the twelfth century on the site of the Roman settlement of **Mariana.** The church and the nearby excavation site are worth a special trip (see page 98). It is only another 3km to the seaside resort of Mariana-Plage.

Just past **Casamozza**, the N193 turns west, and carries on through the central mountains to Ajaccio (133km; see route 5). But the present route continues southward along the N198 coast road, which crosses the Golo and runs along the edge of **Castagniccia**. Although mountainous, the region is both fertile and populous, and is worth a trip for its own sake (see page 117). There are numerous villages along the slopes to the right. To the left is the continuation of the flat coastal plain, which is nowadays increasingly devoted to agriculture.

There are several turnings into Castagniccia along the way. The first of these is the turning for Vescovato, 2km out of Casamozza. 5km further on is the turning for Castellare-di-Casinca, while to the left a small road leads down to the beach at Anghione. After another 4km, the road arrives at **Folelli**, where it crosses the Fium' Alto. Again, there is a left turn for the beach at San Pellegrino and a right turn leading up into Castagniccia.

Both the road and the mountains come closer to the shore during the next 8km to **Moriani-Plage**. Because it is so close to the mountains, Moriani is an ideal resort for those who wish to combine a beach holiday with trips to the interior.

Travellers with less time may nonetheless wish to make a mini-detour through Castagniccia. One recommended route is from Moriani via San Nicolao to Cervione, where the D71 leads back to Prunete (6km). **Prunete** is 5km along the coast road from Moriani. Its artificial harbour at Port de Campoloro is gradually increasing in importance.

During the next 18km section to Aléria, the mountains of Campagniccia retreat into the distance. The road runs along a

Wine from Corsican vineyards is excellent, but almost unknown outside the island

broad coastal plain that is crossed by many rivers. The biggest of these is the Tavignano, which comes down from Lac de Nino on Monte Tozzo in the western mountains, and runs into the sea near Aléria. The other rivers include the Alisani, the Alistro, the Bravone and the Arena. It is a region where the forest and the *maquis* have been cleared to make way for agriculture. The road passes through vineyards and fields full of vegetables.

8km south of Prunete, the road goes to the left of the Alistro lighthouse, which is raised up and at some distance from the coast. The stone-pines are now accompanied by cork oaks, which are the dominant trees in the south of the island. South of the Bravone there is another lighthouse on the left, which is part of a military installation.

About 5km before Aléria, the road turns inland to bypass the Etang de Diane, where the Roman fleets once anchored. This coastal lagoon has particularly salty water and is noticeably calm. It possesses some marvellous stretches of beach.

Just before the road crosses the Tavignano, it meets a crossroads at **Cateraggio**. The road to the left goes down to the shore at Plage de Padulone. The road to the right is the N200 road to Corte (48km), which runs up along the valley of the Tavignano.

The river meanders through some impressive gorges. The road is good, but the tourists are few, making it ideal for a quiet excursion. There are picnic sites, bathing places and camping facilities. 18km before Corte, the road crosses an old bridge past a lovely old church that goes back to AD 1002.

The present village of **Aléria** (40m) is situated on a small rocky outcrop just south of the Tavignano. It is even smaller than its population of 800 would suggest. It was founded in the thirteenth century, and first became important as a bishopric. In the fifteenth century the Genoese built Fort Matra to defend it. But the original site of Aléria goes back to pre-Roman times (see page 100).

The area to the south of Aléria was once a swamp that extended almost as far as Solenzara (32km). Three rivers flowed through it on their way to the sea: the Tavignano, the Fium' Orbo and the Travo. In the meantime, however, most of the land has been reclaimed for agricultural purposes.

The road swings inland again to bypass another lagoon called the Etang d'Urbino. After 15km it arrives at **Ghisonaccia**, which is 4km from the coast, in the centre of a heavily cultivated area. There is a side-road leading down to the beach and to an old tower at Vignale. There is also a turning to the right along the D344, which goes inland along the valley of the **Fium' Orbo** via **Ghisoni** (27km) to **Vivario** (another 20km), which is on the main road between Bastia and Ajaccio (see route 5). It passes through two fascinating gorges called the **Défilé de l'Inzecca** and the **Défilé de Strette**.

Meanwhile, the coast road continues southward in a straight line towards Solenzara (17km). It passes the Etang de Palo and a military airport on the left. On the right the foothills come closer again, and behind them more mountains appear, including the jagged profile of the **Aiguilles de Bavella**. So impressive are they that even the most fanatic beach-lover will be tempted inland.

The road crosses to **Solenzara** over the river of the same name. Solenzara has developed into a lively seaside resort, though the main beach is back on the north side of the river. The remains of an old Roman road have been found in the vicinity. It is also worth making a short journey up the hillside to the nearby viewing point of La Penna (8km).

At the northern end of Solenzara, just south of the river bridge, there is a turning along the D268 to Zonza (39km), which forms

the first part of a suggested detour through the mountain region of
Bavella. The route returns to Porto-Vecchio (another 40km)
along the D368 (see page 158). Both parts of the route are so
beautiful that this detour is a must for all travellers between
Solenzara and Porto-Vecchio. However, the direct coast route is
beautiful too, so it is probably worth combining both routes to
make a round trip.

The east coast so far has been unlike the rest of Corsica. But
the 20km section from Solenzara to the Col de Parata is much
more Corsican in flavour. There is *maquis* everywhere, and the
road follows the irregularities of the steep, rocky shoreline. In
some places it has even been cut out of the cliff, while
occasionally there are small sandy beaches below.

At **Favone** there is a somewhat larger beach, where brightly-
painted fishing boats mingle with the pleasure boats. 4km further
south, there is another good beach at the mouth of the Tarco. The
 road crosses the mouth of the Conca, and passes a rocky headland crowned by a Genoese fort. It front of it there is yet another
sandy beach.

The road turns inland here, and crosses a rocky outcrop via
 the **Col de Parata** (44m). The red rocks and red soil match the
red trunks of the cork oaks. They may combine with the red of the
sunset to create a beautifully romantic scene.

The road soon arrives at **Ste Lucie de Porto-Vecchio** on
the River Cavo, which is 15km north of Porto-Vecchio. One can
turn right here along the D168, which runs along the course of the
Cavo up into the mountains. A second right turn off it leads to the
small hamlet of **Conca**, which is at the south-eastern end of a
famous mountain path called the Grande Randonnée or GR20.
This path goes all the way across the island from Calenzana in the
north-western region of Balagne, passing the Col de Bavella
towards the south-eastern end.

One can also turn left along the D168, which leads down to
Pinarello (4km) on the coast. The Gulf of Pinarello is one of the
most beautiful bays on the whole island, with its white sands and
clear blue water, enclosed by dense green forest. The small coast
road goes south past more lovely bays and beaches, including St
Cyprien, Cala Rossa and Stagnolo on the north side of the Gulf of
Porto-Vecchio, until it eventually arrives at Porto-Vecchio itself.

Meanwhile the main N198 road follows the direct route to Porto-
Vecchio. To the left of the road is the hamlet of **Torre**, which is
named after the nearby Bronze Age tower (*torre*). This is just one

Porto-Vecchio is surrounded by lovely beaches

of the countless prehistoric remains that are found all over the southern part of the island .

Just before **Ste Trinité** there is a brief glimpse of the Gulf of Porto-Vecchio, thought by some to be the most beautiful bay in the Mediterranean. The scenery around Porto-Vecchio is peppered with rocks and outcrops, which are typical of southern Corsica. The land is cultivated with vineyards and olive groves.

Porto-Vecchio itself is an important centre for the export of cork products, which are obtained from the cork-oak forests in the surrounding areas. It is also the most popular tourist centre on Corsica's east coast. Immediately to the south of Porto-Vecchio is the rocky Chiappa Peninsula, which is surrounded by lovely beaches such as the Plage de Palombaggia and the beautiful bay of **Sta Giulia**. These can be reached via side- roads off the N198.

The route continues along the final section of east coast towards Bonifacio at the island's southern tip. The scenery remains strikingly different from that further up the coast. The countryside is hilly and covered in rocky outcrops like those along the southern part of the west coast. These bare crags have been eroded and pitted into bizarre shapes that tower up out of the *maquis* and the woodlands on the hillsides. Some of the hills have been planted with vineyards.

About half-way to Bonifacio, 2km beyond the **Col d'Arésia** (68m), there is an interesting little chapel by the side of the road. Another 2km further on, there is a distant view of the **Uomo di Cagna** ('Man of Cagna'; 1,215m) — a mountain to the west, which is crowned by an enormous rock.

The road passes close to the Gulf of Santa Manza, which alas is scarcely visible from the road. To get a better view, one should turn left along the D60 and go as far as the point where it crosses the D58 from Bonifacio to the bay itself. The Gulf of Santa Manza is especially popular with divers.

The road becomes twisty again for the last 6km after the **Col de Parmentile** (43m). Granite has now been replaced totally by chalk, and the landscape is covered in white dust, especially during the dry summer months.

The road is flanked by olive trees and wild oleander as it makes the final steep descent to the port of **Bonifacio**. The town is an amazingly colourful sight, the bright pastel shades of the café awnings along the quay forming a sharp contrast to the white sails and the fishing boats on the deep blue waters of the harbour. The port is surrounded by greenish-white cliffs, and is dominated by the grim battlements of the citadel.

4 THE SOUTHERN WEST COAST

Bonifacio • Sartène • Propriano • Ajaccio (140km)

The coastline to the south-west of the island is particularly beautiful. The route leaves **Bonifacio** on the N198 Porto-Vecchio road. The road climbs the **Col de Foce de Lera** (90m), and then forks near the top. The route bears left here along the N196 for Sartène (52km) and Ajaccio (another 86km).

The road runs quickly through orchards and olive groves to the **Col d'Arbia** (138m), where there is a beautiful view of Bonifacio and across the strait to Sardinia. The indented coastline of southern Corsica stretches out ahead. There will be more views of this over the next 27km.

The road drops steeply and crosses the many streams that run into the Gulf of Ventilegne. It then climbs steeply again to the **Col de la Testa** (68m), which is 15km from Bonifacio. There is a turning here along the D859, which goes via Figari and Sotta to Porto-Vecchio.

The road goes past the fjord-like **Gulf of Figari** and through the village of Pianotolli. Then there are two turnings for the small wine-producing village of **Monacia**. (The south of Corsica produces some good wines.) The scenery is becoming more typically Corsican, with *maquis* and forest interspersed with bare granite crags.

The road begins to climb again, and soon comes to the first of three viewing points that follow in close succession. Travellers should stop here and take a good look at the **Lion of Roccapina**. Ahead to the left is a massive rocky ridge that towers above the Gulf of Roccapina. It has a row of three peaks, of which the left peak is topped by a Genoese lookout tower, while the right peak looks like a recumbent lion with its head raised up. The lion remains visible for the next 3km as the road goes over the **Col de Coralli**.

Just as the road comes close to the lion, it suddenly veers inland as if in fright, and runs along the hillside above the course of the River Ortolo. After 5km it crosses the river and begins to

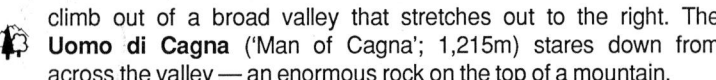

climb out of a broad valley that stretches out to the right. The **Uomo di Cagna** ('Man of Cagna'; 1,215m) stares down from across the valley — an enormous rock on the top of a mountain.

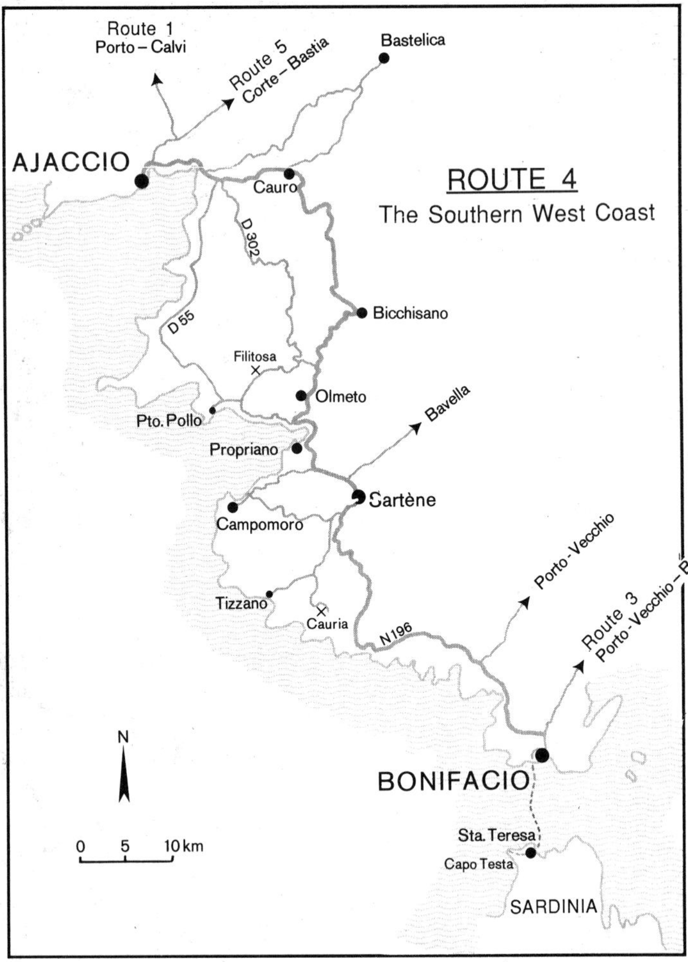

It is 16km further to Sartène; the road continues northwards, bypassing the south-western corner of Corsica. This is a region of forested valleys and *maquis*-covered hills. There are occasional smallholdings surrounded by meadows and fields, and countless

The coast near Porto/Piana

Algajola from the beach

Church at Patrimonio

The peaks of Roccapina

small rivers. The coast is irregular and rocky apart from a few small sandy bays, but is a real paradise for divers.

The south-west of Corsica is a marvellous area for anyone who is interested in archaeology. There are two Megalithic sites at Palaggiu and Fontenaccia, with menhirs and dolmens, and one Torrean site at Alo-Bisucce. These can be reached via the D48 road through the **Tizzano Valley**, which comes off the main road at the top of the **Col d'Albitrina** (290m), 2½km before Sartène. The D48 goes all the way down to Tizzano on the coast (17km), and meets a cross-route to the Gulf of Valinco — the bay where Propriano lies.

Sartène is the most traditionally Corsican town on the whole island, and visitors should stop here for at least 2 hours. The town is described in the section on Propriano). It clings to the hillside about 300m above the valley floor, and affords a marvellous view along the next part of the route to Propriano (13km) and the sea. And there is also a view up into the mountains inland.

As the road drops steeply from Sartène into the valley, there is a brief glimpse of the Bavella mountains, far to the west. The road reaches the bottom 6km from Sartène, and there is a turning along the D268 to Ste Lucie de Tallano.

The N196 bears left along the course of the Rizzanèse, whose

banks are covered in poplars and willows. In a meadow to the left
are two menhirs known as *Frate e Sora* ('Brother and Sister').
They go back to about 2000 BC, and are just one of the many prehistoric sites to be found in this region. The road crosses the river
and climbs over the Col de Santa Giulia into **Propriano** on the
Gulf of Valinco — the main tourist centre in south-west Corsica.

The N196 continues in a wide curve around the end of the bay,
and then turns inland towards the mountains. It is now 73km to
Ajaccio, and the section which follows is particularly scenic. The
road is good and fast, in spite of the many bends, and there are
many lovely views down towards the coast. The first of these
views is across the Gulf of Valinco and all along its southern
shore to a tower on a rocky point called the Punte de Campomoro.

5km out of Propriano there is a left turn along the D157, which
goes off along the north shore of the bay to Porto Pollo (14½km),
passing above a row of lovely beaches known as Marina d'Olmeto
or **Olmeto-Plage**. The road continues further along the coast,
eventually rejoining the N196 near Ajaccio (see below).

The N196 climbs for 4km up the hillside to **Olmeto** (360m) — a
pretty little village high up among the olive groves. The deep
valley drops away to the right. On a rocky platform on the
opposite slope are the ruins of the thirteenth-century Castello
della Rocca. This belonged to the famous della Rocca family —
Corsican nobles who led many of the struggles against Genoese
oppression. Just north of the village, there is an old ruined
monastery to the left of the road. The forests around are a popular
area for hunting wild boar.

The road climbs for another 4km to the **Col de Celaccia**
(582m). There is a left turn here for **Filitosa** which is by far the
most important prehistoric site on Corsica (see page 170).

The N196 winds on for another 10km to **Bicchisano**, which
has a white church that can be seen for many miles around. There
is a right turn here along the D420, which goes across the
mountains via Aullène and Quenza to Zonza (41km), forming the
middle section of the bus route between Ajaccio and Porto-
Vecchio.

The N196 drops down to cross the River Taravo, which comes
down from Monte Grosso near the Col de Verde and runs into the
Gulf of Valinco near Porto Pollo. The road runs through groves of
eucalyptus trees, while the mountain slopes around are covered
with forest and *maquis*. The road climbs again as it approaches
Grosseto.

Hotel du Cap, Porticcio

From Grosseto it is worth making a short detour of 3km through **Ste Marie-Siché** (500m). This small village is beautifully situated overlooking the valley of the Salice, and has associations with the great Corsican freedom-fighter Sampiero Corso. One can still see the house where his mother was born, though it has been somewhat altered since those times. His old castle is now in ruins, but still contains a statue of him. Also of interest is the little old church at the entrance to the village, with its lattice-work tower. The way back to the N196 is along the D83, which comes down from Zicavo.

The N196 climbs up the hillside to the **Col de St Georges** (747m). 1½km before the top, there is a brief glimpse of the little church of Ste Marie-Siché down to the left (see above), beckoning travellers that come down the pass from the north.

During the 7km descent to Cauro, there is an unexpected view of the sea, and high rocky mountains can be seen ahead in the distance. The rich vegetation is due to the westerly winds in the winter, which bring heavy rain to the west of the mountains. Every now and then a ruined castle can be seen poking through the forest. These castles once belonged to Corsican noblemen.

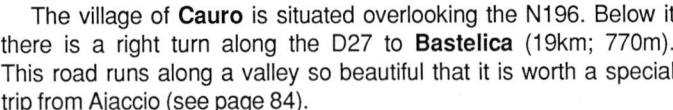

The village of **Cauro** is situated overlooking the N196. Below it there is a right turn along the D27 to **Bastelica** (19km; 770m). This road runs along a valley so beautiful that it is worth a special trip from Ajaccio (see page 84).

It is only 22km more to the town of Napoléon's birth. In the meantime there is a marvellous view across the Gulf of Ajaccio, with the Iles Sanguinaires just visible beyond. About half-way along, just before the Col de Seghia (46m), there is a left turn along the D55 to the popular seaside resort of **Porticcio** (6km). This road continues southwards along the coast, and eventually comes out at Propriano. This forms a delightful alternative to the N196 between Propriano and Ajaccio.

For the last few kilometres before **Ajaccio**, the N196 crosses the broad river valley of the Gravone. As the road circles the airport, one already has a feeling of bustle and prosperity, with the town clearly visible across the bay.

5 THROUGH THE MOUNTAINS

Ajaccio • Vizzavona • Corte • Ponte-Leccia • Bastia/Calvi (153km)

This route runs overland through the mountains of central Corsica. Both road and rail routes tend to keep to the valleys and lower slopes, but there are still some magnificent views. There are forests of chestnut, beech and pine, *maquis* slopes and bare granite peaks. The valleys sometimes form deep gorges with fast-flowing rivers and streams. The first half of the route to Corte is particularly beautiful.

Foot passengers are strongly recommended to go by train. The little red diesel chugs slowly up the line, whistling loudly at the entrance to each of the many tunnels on the way. The line passes over several viaducts that give one a feeling of flying. There is yet further excitement when the train meets goats or pigs on the track and has to whistle to shoo them away.

The N193 road is a good one, and it competes with the railway along the whole length of the route. Which of the two goes higher? — the road mostly. Which has more bends? — why, the road, of course, and the coach drivers lay into them with gusto! Which has more loops? — undoubtedly the railway. Which has the best views? — that is impossible to judge.

It is only 49km — a third of the total distance — from **Ajaccio** to the highest point on the route, the **Col de Vizzavona** (1,163m). The railway follows the valley of the Gravone for most of this section; but the road only joins it after 10km before climbing over a small pass called the **Col de Carazzi** (204m), which is 18km from Ajaccio.

From here the road flattens out then becomes gradually steeper. It climbs 84m in the next 10km, 110m in the following 5km to below Tavera, and then 242m in the 7km section to Bocognano. The landscape is dominated by high mountains on either side, including Monte d'Oro (2,389m) ahead to the left, and Monte Renoso (2,352m) on the right. The latter forms the source of the Gravone — the main river through the valley.

Bocognano is an ideal destination for day-trippers from

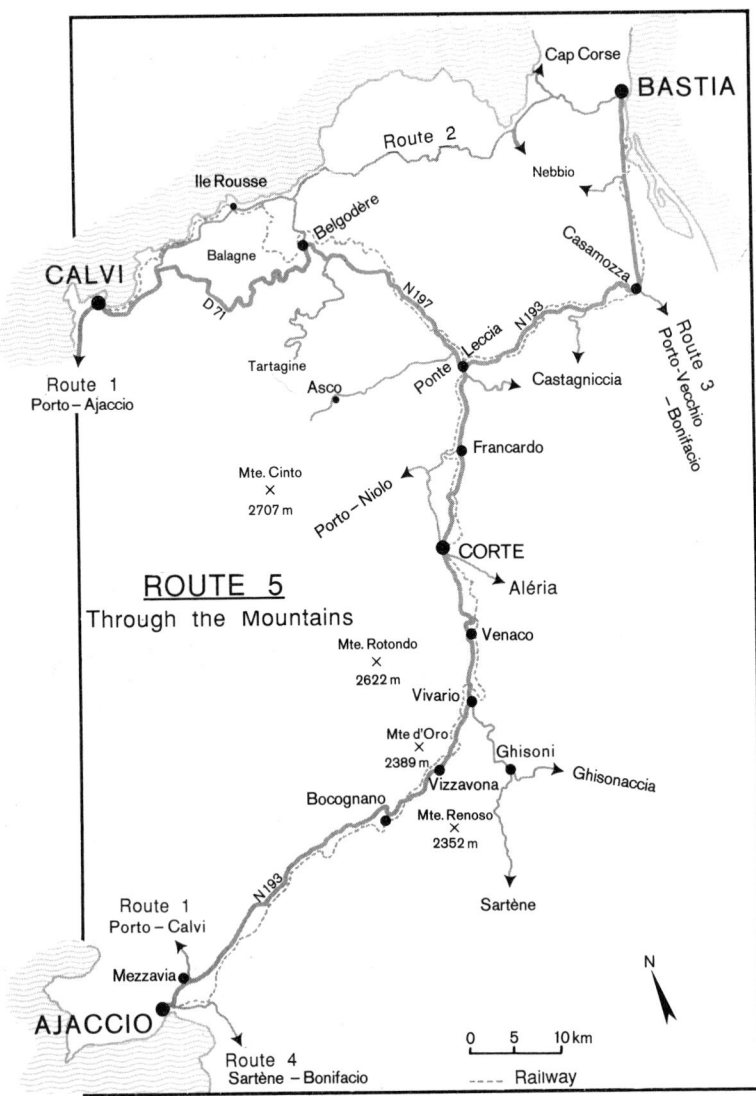

coastal resorts around Ajaccio who would like a taste of some
cool mountain air. It is 40km away from Ajaccio and 640m above
sea level. Its setting is beautiful among the chestnut forests on

the valley slope.

Immediately before the village, there is a right turn along the D27 to **Bastelica** (19km). This goes over the **Col de la Scalella** (1,193m), from which there are some magnificent views. About 3km along, there is a footpath going up the side of the Punta al Collo (1,240m). One walks alongside a fast mountain stream, and after 15 minutes arrives at an impressive waterfall called the *Voile de la Mariée* or 'Bridal Veil'.

Day-trippers are also recommended to include Vizzavona in their itinerary, as it is only another 12km further on. The N193 drops down slightly to cross the Gravone, and then makes the final steep ascent to the **Col de Vizzavona**. It passes a ruined Genoese castle on the left, with the nearby peak of Monte d'Oro behind it. Meanwhile, the railway disappears into a tunnel, and emerges at **Vizzavona** itself (906m), 3km beyond the top of the pass. The road runs along the forest-covered slopes above the village. The Forêt de Vizzavona is a much-prized area of mixed coniferous and deciduous forest.

Vizzavona is an ideal centre for a walking holiday. There are numerous footpaths among the forests around (no need to worry about wild boars!), past gorges and waterfalls, and up the slopes of Monte d'Oro to beyond the tree line.

The most popular local walk is to the Cascade des Anglais ('Waterfall of the English'), where the River Agone plunges down the side of Monte d'Oro. This can be reached via a small road which comes off the main road at a hamlet called La Foce between Vizzavona and the top of the pass. The road ends at a bridge over the Agone called Pont Cassagneau. Just before the bridge, there is a footpath to the left leading up to the waterfall (15 minutes); just over the bridge, there is a footpath to the right going back down to Vizzavona (30 minutes). This is actually part of the famous Grande Randonnée or GR20, which runs all the way across Corsica, from Calenzana in the north-west, via Monte d'Oro and Vizzavona, to Conca in the south-east of the island.

During the next 31km to Corte (396m), both road and rail follow a winding course which goes mostly downhill. The first section passes above the Vecchio Gorges, going right through the middle of Corsica's great national park. At **Tattone** there is a modern sanatorium, which though ugly in itself is in an ideal situation among the mountains.

7km from Vizzavona, the road crosses another pass called the **Col de la Serra** (807m). There is a left turn here along the D344

Roadside hotel, Ghisoni

 to Ghisoni (20km), going on to Ghisonaccia (another 27km; see route 3) via a series of gorges along the Fium' Orbo. **Ghisoni** itself is beautifully situated on a forested slope; it offers some marvellous walks and some good local wines.

From the Col de la Serra the N193 begins a dramatic descent through Vivario, dropping 400m within 6km. Just beyond the top of the pass, there is a magnificent view to the north along the Vecchio Valley. The railway goes out a long way in front before turning back in an enormous loop to arrive at Vivario, 150m beneath. It then makes a further dramatic loop, and comes back past Vivario along the opposite side of the valley.

The road descends the 2km to **Vivario** (650m) via several hairpins. The village itself is situated on a shelf part-way up the mountainside. The village fountain sports a statue of the goddess Diana — an appropriate symbol of the good hunting that can be found in the forests around.

During the next 4km, the road drops steeply via a dramatic series of hairpins, and eventually bridges the Vecchio at a height of only 400m. The railway cannot match this, and in spite of the enormous loops it has made, it is much higher than the road by this stage. It crosses the valley via an enormous viaduct, 140m long and 96m high, which was built by Eiffel of Eiffel Tower fame.

Venaco, a popular mountain resort

Both road and rail follow the course of the Vecchio for a short distance, but the river soon swings off to the east, and the route climbs out of the valley up to **Venaco** (565m). Venaco is the centre of a group of scattered villages, and is a popular summer mountain resort.

The road climbs steeply again over the **Col de Bellan-** **granajo** (723m), where there is a magnificent view from the top. The scenery has been gradually changing since Vivario: thick forests have been replaced by *maquis* with occasional clumps of olive or chestnut trees; some slopes have been planted with orchards or vineyards; and there are a few patches of rough grass, which serve as pasture for sheep and goats. In short, the landscape is drier and more open — a sign that the road has crossed over to the east side of the island, which is sheltered from the effects of the moist winter westerlies.

The road begins a long descent, and after 12km arrives at the small town of **Corte** (396m), which is situated on the edge of the Tavignano Valley. There is an imposing fortress on the steep, rocky summit overlooking the old town. Corte has a chapter to itself .

There are several important routes out of Corte. The N200 goes south-east along the Tavignano Valley to Aléria on the coast (see route 3). The D18 goes due north to join the D84, which goes west through the gorgeous mountain scenery of Niolo). The present route continues north-east along the N193 Bastia road, and eventually joins the lower course of the Golo. The Golo and the Tavignano form the northern and southern limits of the Castagniccia region.

The next part of the route is the 24km section along the N193 from Corte to Ponte Leccia. First the road crosses another pass called the **Col de San Quilico** (539m). This is an easy climb, thanks to the newly-made road. The road begins to descend, making a wide loop towards **Sovéria**; it then swings across to the right-hand side of the valley, while the railway crosses to the left. Both continue down the valley to cross the great River Golo just before Francardo.

In the meantime, there is a lovely view across the valley from the railway to the village of **Omessa**, which is 2km to the east of the N193. Its most interesting features are the Baroque church tower and the one-time monastery (Château de Bellevue), which now houses the local district offices.

Just before **Francardo** (261m) there is a left turn along the D84 (see above), which goes westwards up the course of the Golo through Niolo, and eventually arrives at Porto on the west coast (see route 1). Francardo itself is important for its large sawmill and its brickworks.

The N193 crosses the Golo, while the railway forms a loop and crosses it 2km further upstream. Both of them go downstream along the left side of the valley towards Ponte Leccia (9km). The route now leaves the highest of the mountains behind, passing a spur of the Monte Cinto range on the left and the hills of Castagniccia to the right. There are no more pines, and the climate becomes noticeably warmer.

Ponte Leccia lies on a small plain at the confluence of several rivers. It is an important road and railway junction, with routes going to Bastia and Calvi respectively (see below). There is another road turning along the D71, which goes due east towards **Morosaglia** (14km). At the small hamlet of **Stretta** just beyond here is the house where the great Corsican hero Pasquale Paoli was born; it has now been turned into a museum. The D71 continues through lovely scenery to **Piedicroce** (another 16km) — the main village of the region of **Castagniccia** (see page 117).

Ponte Leccia to Bastia

The Bastia railway and the N193 both turn north-eastwards from Ponte Leccia, and follow the course of the Golo for the next 26km to Casamozza, passing to the north of Castagniccia (see above).

The most interesting place on the route is **Ponte Nuovo**, 8km from Ponte Leccia. The name Ponte Nuovo ('new bridge') refers not to the present modern bridge, built in 1958, but to the old Genoese one, much of which has survived to this day. It originally had five arches, but the two middle ones have fallen into the river. At the northern end of the village is a large pyramid-shaped monument, commemorating the Battle of Ponte Nuovo in 1769, in which the Corsicans under Pasquale Paoli were defeated by the French, thus ending their great hopes of freedom.

At **Casamozza** the N193 joins the eastern coastal route for the final 20km to **Bastia** (see route 3).

Ponte Leccia to Calvi

This route goes north-west from Ponte Leccia along the N197 to Calvi. The first 33km to Belgodère are through a wild landscape of mountains, forests and *maquis*. There is a junction 2km north of Ponte Leccia, where a minor road goes left into the beautiful **Asco Valley** (see page 147). 24km further on, there is another left turn along a small road into the **Forêt de Tartagine** (see page 138).

From **Belgodère** there are at least two possible routes to Calvi. The direct route is along the N197 via Ile Rousse (15km) and the north coast (see route 2). Alternatively, one can turn left along the D71, which goes through the beautiful mountain region of **Balagne** (see page 131).

The Calvi railway follows the road for the first part of the route. This is followed by a section of loops and tunnels, before the railway rejoins the N197 on the coast, which it follows from Ile Rousse to **Calvi**.

6 AJACCIO

Imperial City on the West Coast

With a population of 50,000, Ajaccio is Corsica's second-largest town. It is the capital of the French *département* of Corse-du-Sud, and was the capital of the whole island before its division into two *départements*. It is situated by the side of a large bay on the island's irregular west coast, at roughly the same latitude as Rome. Because it faces southwards and is sheltered by mountains to the north, it is unusually mild in winter. Thus, even before the tourist boom, it was already popular as an all-year-round holiday resort.

Ajaccio is a very friendly and hospitable town, combining the functions of seaport and seaside resort. The presence of the sea is all-pervasive, and the ever-present breezes combine the perfumes of the *maquis* with the salty tang of the sea.

One is continually reminded of the fact that Napoléon was born here — hence its French nickname *le Berceau d'Empéreur* or 'the Emperor's Cradle'. There are permanent illuminations of the kind that are normally only mounted at Christmas, and many of these are designed to represent things which belonged to Napoléon such as his crown, his general's hat and his sword. There is often an impressive *son et lumière* performance in the evening.

Ajaccio was originally a Roman settlement on a hill to the north of the present town. Much evidence has been uncovered from this period, including the ruins of a Roman fortification known as Castel-Vecchio. The town's Roman name was Adjacium or 'resting place'. But when the Saracens began to raid the coast in the tenth century, the inhabitants could no longer rest here and fled into the mountains.

When the Genoese took over, they built a new fortress not far from the old Roman settlement, and a town grew up around it. The townspeople suffered greatly under the oppressive rule of the Genoese, especially following their support of the Corsican rebellion under Raffé de Leca in 1454–5. In 1492, following the period when the island was handed over to the Bank of St George,

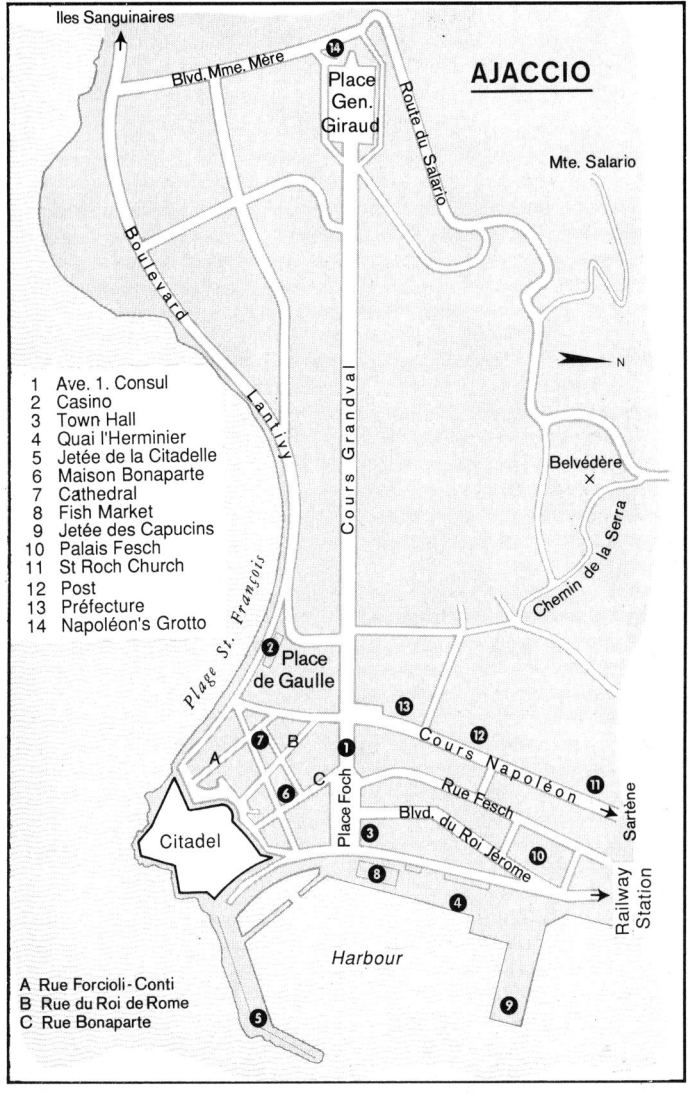

the Genoese built a new town by the harbour, but refused to let the Corsicans live there.

In 1553 the great Corsican freedom-fighter Sampiero Corso

captured the town in a surprise attack, and it came under the
protection of the French. A year later the French began to build
their citadel on the headland. But only 5 years after this, the
Genoese recaptured the town, and it was not until 1768 that the
French gained permanent control.

At that time the town had a population of only 4,000. The fact
that it had grown to more than ten times that number by 1900
owes much to the efforts made to save the island from economic
ruin. The Corsican name for the town is Aiacciu or Ajax, and the
inhabitants call it 'Aye-atch'.

The old town is clustered around the citadel; the industrial
areas are out to the east, while the modern residential areas are
spread out to the north and the west. They have taken much of
the town's traditional atmosphere away, but have placed it firmly
in the twentieth century.

Ajaccio is linked to the French mainland by air and sea routes.
There are bus services to all parts of the island, and trains to
Bastia and Calvi. The town has its own bus transport network,
which includes services to the Tour de la Parata and the nearby
coastal resort of Porticcio.

Ajaccio's central square is the Place Général de Gaulle, which
is situated at the meeting point of the town's two main
thoroughfares, the Cours Napoléon and the Cours Grandval. The

Ajaccio from the harbour

name of the square is somewhat inappropriate in view of the town's Napoleonic associations. There is a statue of Napoléon on horseback and surrounded by his four brothers. There is also a fountain, which is surrounded by a flower display and is lit up at night. The casino is close by on a promenade overlooking the shore, and there are several cafés where one may imbibe *pastis* in true Corsican style.

The Avenue Premier Consul leads from the Place Général de Gaulle to the Place Maréchal Foch, where the **Town Hall** is situated on the left-hand side. It contains the tourist information office on the ground floor and the **Napoleonic Museum** on the first floor (the entrance ticket is also valid for the Palais Fesch — see below). The square opens out onto the main harbour. Its two main piers are the Quai l'Herminier, where the passenger boats dock, and the Quai Napoléon. It is flanked by two breakwaters: the Jetée des Capucins on the left, and the Jetée de la Citadelle on the right, which affords a marvellous view of the town with the mountains behind.

The main part of the old town is sandwiched between the Place Général de Gaulle and the citadel, which is closed to the public. The three main streets are the Rue Bonaparte, the Rue du Roi de Rome and the Rue Forcioli-Conti. On the corner of the Rue du Roi de Rome and the Rue St Charles which crosses it is the four-teenth-century **Church of St John the Baptist**, which once housed Ajaccio's oldest monastic community.

Also in the Rue St Charles is the **Maison Bonaparte**, so named because Napoléon was born here. The house is no different from any other seventeenth-century residence, and is distinguished only by the Bonaparte coat of arms above the door and a memorial plaque on the wall. The greatest Corsican of them all was born here on 15 August 1769, the second son of a lawyer called Carlo Bonaparte. In 1793 the house was set on fire by supporters of Pasquale Paoli, but the family had already fled to France.

The **cathedral** is close by in the Rue Forcioli-Conti. It still contains the white marble font in which Napoléon was baptised. The high altar of white and coloured marble was donated by one of Napoléon's sisters. The façade and the large dome above it seem plain and rather ponderous in comparison with the brightly decorated interior. Known in Corsican as *U Domu*, the cathedral was built between 1554 and 1593, and its ground plan is in the form of a Greek cross. It was dedicated to Our Lady of Mercy, the

Palm-lined streets, Ajaccio

patron saint of the town, who is commemorated on 18 March.

Also on Rue Forcioli-Conti and towards the citadel is **St Erasmus' Church**, which originally belonged to the Jesuits. After their expulsion it was used for various secular purposes until 1815, when it was rededicated to seafarers. Every year on St Erasmus' Day (2 June) there is a special procession through Ajaccio. The Boulevard Lantivy runs from the citadel along the promenade of the Plage St François.

Along the harbour front from the citadel, the fish market provides some interesting insights into Corsican life. One can continue from here through the narrow streets of the old town. The

washing hangs on lines overhead, and the balconies contain
birdcages and pots full of flowers, while on some of them the old
toilet outbuilding is still clearly to be seen.

Opposite the Jetée des Capucins, where the old town ends, is
the **Palais Fesch**, which stands between the Boulevard du Roi   ⌘
Jérôme and the Rue Fesch. This large and complex building goes
back to the time of Napoléon III, and houses the many treasures
bequeathed to the town by Napoléon's uncle, Cardinal Fesch.

The left wing of the building contains the **Musée Fesch** —   ⌘
the cardinal's collection of 1,200 paintings, of which some are on
permanent and some on temporary display. Apart from the Louvre
in Paris, it is France's most important collection of Italian
masterpieces. Also in this wing is a library containing 40,000
volumes, 8,000 of which belonged to the cardinal.

In the right wing of the Palais Fesch is the **Chapelle**   ⌘
Impériale, where several members of the Bonaparte family are
buried. Above the main altar is the crucifix that Napoléon brought
back to his mother from his Egyptian campaign.

Above the Rue Fesch on the Cours Napoléon are St Roch's
Oratory and the modern **Church of St Roch**, which was built in   ⌘
1895 and contains stained-glass windows from 1956. Going back
towards the Place Général de Gaulle, one passes the town's main
post office on the left.

Turning right at the Place Général de Gaulle, one enters the
Cours Grandval. The town's main boulevard, it is lined by avenues
of palms and plane trees. It turns into the Cours du Général
Leclerc, which eventually leads up to the Place du Général
Giraud. In the middle of the square is a copy of the famous statue
of Napoléon in front of Les Invalides in Paris. To the left is a grotto
where Napoléon played as a child, and which these days is a
popular meeting place for young lovers.

There are two possible ways back to the Place Général de
Gaulle. One of these is to go down to the shore along the
Boulevard Madame Mère and to return along the promenade. The
other possibility is to turn right up the Route du Salario and to
come back along the hillside via a lookout point known appropriately as Belvédère.

Visitors are also recommended to go on a tour of the hillside
behind the town. It is about 10km long, and includes the lookout   ⌘
point on **Monte Salario** (311m) to the south-west and the
former Bonaparte country residence of Milelli to the north-west.

Milelli is also the location for events such as the Ajaccio Music

The Iles Sanguinaires

Festival in the summer. The direct route to it is via a road that goes left (signposted) off the Cours Napoléon, just past the station. Information about this and other cultural activities is available from the cultural centre on the Place Général de Gaulle.

Also near the station are the marina and a moped hire firm (Miniconi, 21 Boulevard Paoli).

Excursions from Ajaccio

Tour de la Parata (12km)

This old Genoese watchtower stands on top of a 60m high cliff at the end of the long promontory at the northern end of the Gulf of Ajaccio. It is close to the Iles Sanguinaires, and provides some quite magnificent views.

To get there, one travels west along the coast road from the Place Général de Gaulle. 3km from the town centre is the

Chapelle des Grecs, which was built for the Greeks who fled here from Paomina. A little further along is the town's main cemetery, which looks rather like a miniature village.

The **Iles Sanguinaires** ('Blood Islands') are a group of small rocky islands of red granite. The largest of them has a lighthouse at its highest point (80m), while another of them is surmounted by yet another ruined watchtower. The islands are particularly beautiful in the red light of sunset (whence they no doubt got their name), and have come to symbolise Ajaccio. There are boat trips from the Quai Napoléon at Ajaccio (see above)

Pozzo-di-Borgo (13km)
The route goes along the D61, which turns off the Cours Napoléon just past the station. After 7km it arrives at the Bocca di Pruno, where there is a left turn for the Château de la Punta (6km).

The **Punta Pozzo-di-Borgo** (780m) is another 2km further on, and can be reached on foot. There is a radio station at the summit, and the view is one of the finest and most extensive in the whole region. It includes the Gulfs of Ajaccio and Sagone, together with the broad peninsula in between.

The **Château de la Punta** itself was built by the Pozzo-di-Borgo family at the end of the nineteenth century. This delightful little *château* was built in the Louis Quinze style from remnants of the old town hall and the Tuileries in Paris, which had been burned down in 1871. The family mausoleum is situated close by.

Piana and Les Calanches (71km)
See **Cinarca** (below) and route 1.

Pointe de la Castagna (36km)
This excursion goes southwards along the coast of the bay via Porticcio, and returns via an inland route. Tour operators offer coach trips here, though most of them return via the coast road so that tourists may enjoy the beauty of a sunset over the sea.

The route leaves Ajaccio on the N196 Sartène road, then turns right onto the D55 for **Porticcio**. 6km after Porticcio, there is a small road to the right leading to the Tour dell' Isolella, which stands on a headland called the Punte de Sette Nave. The D55 continues along the shore, and after 5¹⁄₂km arrives at **Port de Chiavari**. To the left is an extensive area of woodland called the Forêt de Chiavari.

A small side-road from Port de Chiavari covers the final 6km to

the end of the **Pointe de la Castagna**. From the old tower at
the point, there is a marvellous view of the Gulf of Ajaccio, framed
by the surrounding mountains.

The D55 goes inland from Port de Chiavari, and follows a
winding and rather hilly route to Propriano (another 48km). It
passes a turning for Filitosa (see below), and eventually comes
into the N196, by which one may return to Ajaccio (see route 4).

Filitosa (69km)

Filitosa is the most important prehistoric site in the whole of
Corsica (see page 170). It is 9km from the main N196 Ajaccio-
Sartène road, from which it is signposted 10km south of
Bicchisano (see route 4).

Bocognano and Vizzavona (52km)

These two mountain resorts are described in route 5.

Bastelica (41km)

Bastelica (770m) is situated near the top end of the lovely Prunelli
Valley and at the foot of the Monte Renoso massif. This small
village is becoming increasingly popular with day-trippers, and
there are coach tours laid on from Ajaccio and Propriano.

The D27 road to Bastelica leaves the N196 Ajaccio-Sartène
road at **Cauro** (356m; see route 4). Just before Cauro there is a
small road to the left, leading to the place where Sampiero Corso

Château de la Punta

was brutally murdered in 1567 (see below). There is a memorial stone on the site, which is on the bank of a stream between the villages of Suarelli and Eccica.

The D27 goes through 20km of gorgeous scenery, including forests of chestnut and oak. The road goes over four passes, the first of which is the **Col de Sant' Alberto** (521m), 6½km after Cauro. Shortly afterwards the road goes past a waterfall down below to the right. The passes which follow are the **Col de Marcuccio** (661m), the **Col de Criccheto** (709m) and the **Col de Menta** (762m). Just before Bastelica there is a waterfall to the left called the Cascade d'Aziana. Monte Renoso (2,352m) is clearly visible in the background.

Bastelica itself has an interesting fourteenth-century church. In front of it is a bronze statue of the great sixteenth-century freedom-fighter Sampiero Corso — 'that most Corsican of Corsican heroes'. His birthplace was at nearby Dominicacci; it was burnt down by the Genoese, but has since been reconstructed. The life of Sampiero Corso was so full of passion and suffering that it reads today like a romantic novel or a Shakespearean tragedy.

For a possible alternative route home, one can turn right onto the D3 at a junction between the first two passes on the way back. This is the route usually taken by coaches, and returns via Tolla and Ocana. It passes a large reservoir and hydroelectric power station, and goes near to the Prunelli Gorges.

A Further Excursion

The Cinarca Region

Cinarca is the region to the north of Ajaccio which forms the hinterland to the Gulf of Sagone. It is a fertile area, producing fruit, vegetables, olives and wine. For visitors staying on the coast, it provides a welcome break from swimming or sunbathing on the beach. The scenery is immensely varied, including chestnut and pine forests, *maquis* and green mountain pastures.

The first route of interest is the upland road that winds above the glorious Liscia Valley from Calcatoggio to the scattered community of **Sari-d'Orcino**. (Calcatoggio is just off the D81 coast road, 3km north of the **Col de San Bastiano**, 22km north of Ajaccio and 16km south of Sagone; see route 1.) There is

another road along the north side of the same valley from **Tiuccia** (also on the coast road), but this is less interesting, apart from the ruined castle of the Count of Cinarca, which overlooks Tiuccia itself.

On the other hand, the route from Tiuccia or Sari-d'Orcino to Vico via **Ambiegna** and **Arbori** is really quite outstanding (37km). After Ambiegna the road crosses the valley` of the Liamone, the main river in the region. It runs close to the Liamone both before and after the river crossing at Pont de Truggia.

The main road to Vico is the D70 (13km) from the coastal resort of **Sagone** (see route 1). **Vico** (400m) was at one time a bishopric and the capital of Cinarca, but these days it is rather off the beaten track. It clings to the mountainside above the Liamone Valley, but below the D70 Sagone-Evisa road. Vico was very important in the past, when strong defences were needed to protect it from outsiders. But nowadays outsiders come to gaze at its lovely ancient streets with their romantic old buildings, and to dream of its past glories.

With a population of 2,000, Vico is still larger than any of the coastal resorts between Ajaccio and Calvi, none of which have a resident population of more than 1,000. Vico even has a few wood and metal industries, and is the home of the famous briar pipe. It was the birthplace of Auguste-François Vico, who became governor of Sardinia, and Mgr Casanelli d'Istria, who became bishop of Ajaccio. There is a statue of the latter next to the fountain in the market place.

Just to the south of the town is St Francis' Monastery, which was built in the late fifteenth century by one of the Corsican freedom-fighters. The seventeenth-century extension is still clearly recognisable. The building was partly destroyed at the time of the French Revolution, but was later restored to its original state. The church contains the remains of an old wooden crucifix, which the first monks brought over from Italy, and a wooden tabernacle from about 1700 depicting the four evangelists.

There are some marvellous walks in the forests around, including one to the **Punta alle Cuma** (911m) — a mountain to the south of Vico. It is only an hour's climb away, and provides some glorious views across to the sea.

Another place worth visiting is **Guagno-les-Bains** (480m) — a small health resort with sulphurous springs, 11km due east of Vico along a road through some magnificent scenery. There are turnings off this road leading to two small villages called **Orto** and **Soccia**. Soccia lies in a deep hollow at the foot of the mountains, and has a church with a beautiful fifteenth-century triptych.

Ramblers are recommended to continue on foot to the **Lac de**

Bridge over the River Porto

Creno (1,203m), which is two to three hours' walk from either Orto or Soccia, and is one of the most beautiful lakes on the island. It lies to the north of the summit of **Monte Sant' Eliseo** (1,510m), which belongs to the same range as **Monte Rotundo** (2,622m), Corsica's second-highest mountain.

The D70 passes to the west of Vico over the **Col de St Antoine** (496m), and continues to climb for the next 12km as it goes north-east towards the **Col de Sevi** (1,101m). There is a magnificent view from the top of the pass; the massive grey mountains of central Corsica rise up to the east, while to the west one can see the jagged red cliffs that border the Gulf of Porto.

7km further on, the D70 comes into the D84. If one turns left here, one soon arrives at **Evisa** (2km; see below), beyond which are **Porto** (another 22km; see page 45) and the west coast (26km).

Evisa — Corsica's most popular inland resort

A right turn brings one quickly into a beautiful wooded region called the **Forêt d'Aitone**. There are numerous paths through the forest, one of which leaves the D84 not far from the D70 junction; it goes down to the banks of a mountain stream called the Aitone, and then runs upstream to a group of waterfalls called the Cascades d'Aitone. Another path leaves the road about 1km further on, and climbs up to Belvédère (925m), from which the Aitone can be seen far below.

The D84 climbs steeply for next 10km as it approaches the **Col de Vergio**, which at 1,464m is the highest road pass in Corsica. The top of the pass is covered with Corsican pines, but there is a lookout point just before the top, offering a marvellous view down to the coast. Just over the top, there is another view to the east down the broad valley of the Golo to the Lac de Niolo near Calacuccia, 23km away. To the north is Paglia Orba (2,525m), Corsica's most beautiful peak. A short way down the other side, the road crosses a famous mountain path called the Grande Randonnée or GR20, which is marked out by white-and-red posts. Visitors may care to join the path for a short distance.

Evisa (830m) is Corsica's most popular inland resort, though it has a resident population of barely 600. It is perched high up on a small rocky platform overlooking the confluence of the Aitone and the Porto. It is surrounded by groves of chestnut trees, and

Piana

the viewing point on the mountainside above has been appropriately named La Châtaignerie.

Immediately below Evisa is the famous **Spelunca Gorge**, where the River Porto forces its way through a narrow gap between two cliffs. There is a steep zigzag footpath from Evisa to the bottom of the gorge, 600m below. It leaves the road just past the cemetery at the western end of the village. After about half an hour's climb it arrives at the bottom at the point where the Aitone comes into the Porto. It crosses the Porto via an old Genoese bridge, and turns west to follow the south bank of the river as it rushes down through the gorge.

The river is hemmed in by massive walls of reddish stone, completely bare of vegetation. So inhospitable is the terrain that it seems incredible that the Romans actually managed to build a road through here. They built it extremely well, sometimes hewing it out of the bare rock. It remains there to this day as a lasting reminder of their engineering achievements, though it is admittedly unsuitable for modern vehicles.

It is about half an hour's walk to the western end of the gorge, where a road crosses the river via another old Genoese bridge. For those who wish to have a bathe, there is a suitable spot about ten minutes further on, next to yet another old Genoese bridge. One can of course return on foot via the same route, but the climb is rather exhausting. So some walkers prefer to try their luck at hitching a lift back to Evisa along the road.

The road route from Evisa is very much longer (19km), but it runs through some of the most beautiful scenery in Corsica. The D84 makes a large loop as it climbs down into the valley and crosses the river. It then returns along the south side of the valley. It is 17km from Evisa to the turning for the side-road to the western end of the Spelunca Gorge (2km). Both roads continue to **Porto** (5km).

Not far from Porto is yet another of the incredible sights that Cinarca has to offer. **Les Calanches** are a line of bizarre cliff formations on the south side of the Gulf of Porto between Porto and the small holiday resort of Piana.

Piana is on the D81 coast road, 12km south-west of Porto and 33km north of Sagone (see route 1). It is in a lovely breezy situation 438m above the shore, making it an ideal centre for holidaymakers who prefer to stay away from the beach. There are ample opportunities for walking through the neighbouring woodlands and *maquis*. Of particular interest is the eighteenth-century church of St Mary's, with its beautiful bell tower.

More adventurous motorists may care to try the rather difficult run to **Capo Rosso** (331m) — the red rocky headland that marks the southern end of the Gulf of Porto. It is crowned by a Genoese watchtower, and there are also some magnificent views. The road to the cape then turns southwards, and terminates at the lovely little bay of **Port d'Arone**, 12km away from Piana. Port d'Arone nestles among the rocks at the point where two streams enter the sea; it has about 500m of beach.

On the coast just to the north of Piana is a little cove called the **Anse de Ficajola**, with about 100m of beach. It is only 4km from Piana by road, and can be reached in 50 minutes on foot via a path that turns left off the main Porto road about 1km outside the village. Another path goes off to the right at the same point, leading after a good 2 hours' walk to the ruined fort of Foce d'Orto (989m).

Another 2km further along the same road, and about thirty minutes' walk from Piana, is a restaurant called *Roches Bleues*, which forms a good centre for walks through Les Calanches and the forests around Piana. The view from here of the sunset over the cliffs is an unforgettable experience.

7 BASTIA

North-Eastern Gateway to Corsica

Bastia is situated towards the northern end of the island's eastern shore at the foot of Cap Corse. With a population of 55,000, it is the largest and in many ways the least Corsican town on the island.

Bastia was founded on the site of the Roman settlement of Mantinum, and was originally no more than a small port serving the village of Cardo on the hillside above. But the Genoese recognised the advantages of its proximity to the Italian mainland and its fertile and productive hinterland. And in 1378 they built a massive fort or *bastida* on the headland overlooking the old harbour — hence the origin of the name Bastia. The port grew apace under its protection, and a new settlement grew up around the base of the fort. It was named Terra Nuova ('new land') as opposed to the old original settlement of Terra Vecchia ('old land').

The town continued to flourish under the Genoese. A century later they built enormous battlements and a moat around the new settlement, creating a vast citadel that remains there to this day. Bastia had in the meantime become the seat of the Genoese government, while the bishop had moved his residence here from nearby Mariana.

In the nineteenth century a new port was built to the north of the old one, and further new settlements grew up around it. In the present century the city has expanded southwards, and is becoming increasingly industrial. But it still remains the island's largest port, and the whole town retains a distinctively Genoese quality. Recently, when the island was divided into two *départements*, Bastia quite naturally became the capital of the northern division of Haute-Corse.

Most visitors to Bastia are deposited on the Avenue Maréchal Sébastiani. At the western end is the railway station, to the east the new harbour; the main bus terminals are in the middle on the south side and the main post office is on the north side. The

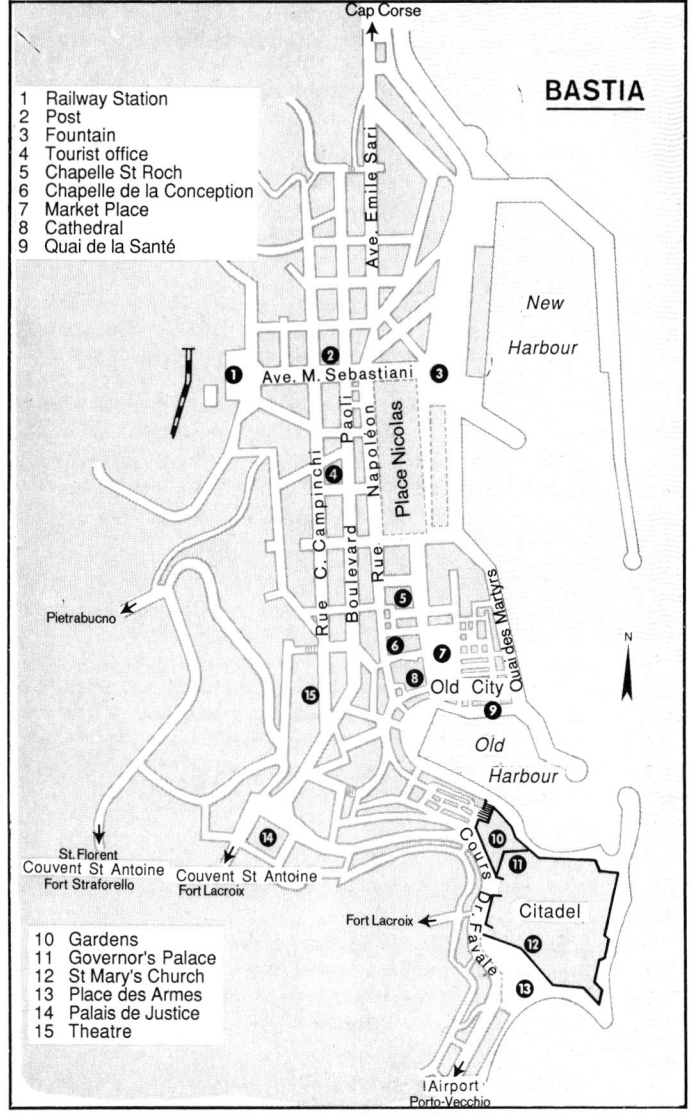

BASTIA

1 Railway Station
2 Post
3 Fountain
4 Tourist office
5 Chapelle St Roch
6 Chapelle de la Conception
7 Market Place
8 Cathedral
9 Quai de la Santé

10 Gardens
11 Governor's Palace
12 St Mary's Church
13 Place des Armes
14 Palais de Justice
15 Theatre

tourist information office is a short distance to the south along the Boulevard Paoli. Visitors are advised to purchase a good town plan here before embarking on a tour of the city.

The suggested tour begins next to the new harbour, where there are fountains and illuminations in the evenings. Immediately behind the harbour is a wide, open square called the Place St Nicolas, which contains a statue of Napoléon and a war memorial.

Visitors are recommended to walk south along the Quai des Martyrs de la Libération, which leads out onto a breakwater in front of the old harbour. The brightly-painted fishing boats and the white sails of the yachts combine to create a colourful scene on the still waters of the harbour. On the other side the waves break on a shingle beach where fishermen throw out their nets.

Behind the harbour are the tall buildings of the old town. There is washing hanging out of the windows above, while the ground floors are occupied by shops, restaurants and cafés, alive with the colours of the sunshades and the sounds of guitar music. Behind all this, the towers of the cathedral are framed by the mountains at the back of the town. There are no modern skyscrapers to mar the town's old-world atmosphere.

Across the harbour to the left is the massive edifice of the **citadel**, which is reached by walking along the Quai de la Santé all the way round the harbour. To get a better view, one should take a flight of steps to the right, and go up past the citadel gardens to the Cours Dr Favale, which is the main road south of the city. To the left is the old main gate to the citadel.

The two modern entrances to the citadel are a little further along. The first is an archway in the battlements. This opens onto a square, to the left of which is the fourteenth-century **Governor's Palace**. Its upper floors are now used as barracks, but the museum on the ground floor is very interesting and well worth a visit. Ahead to the right is the Rue Notre Dame, at the end of which is St Mary's Church on the left. On the right is another gateway leading out again to the Place des Armes, which, since it adjoins the Cours Dr Favale, forms the second way into the citadel. It also provides a good view of the coast to the south.

St Mary's Church was founded in 1495, and for a short time served as the cathedral for the diocese of Mariana. The most interesting feature inside is a fifteenth-century painting of the Assumption of the Virgin Mary, which was moved there from La Canonica at Mariana. In a glass case to the right of it is a silver statue of Mary, which is carried through the streets of the town on

The harbour, Bastia

the Festival of the Assumption on 15 August.

If one turns right on leaving the church, there is another small road to the right along the side of it. On the right just past the church is an ordinary house entrance leading to the **Chapelle Ste-Croix.** From here one can see the back of St Mary's, with its choir and its seventeenth-century lantern-shaped bell tower, which though typical of its day is rather smaller than one might expect.

The interior of the chapel itself looks almost like a Louis Quinze room, with eighteenth-century gold stucco decorations. The building, however, goes back to 1547, and was built to house a black wooden crucifix known as the Christ of Miracles, which is still there to the right of the altar. It is supposed to have been discovered by fishermen, who in 1428 found it floating on the sea surrounded by four lights. It is carried at the head of an annual procession on 3 May, and the local fishermen present the first catch of the year before it.

At the end of the same road, by a modern merchant navy building, there is a marvellous view across the sea. On a clear day Italy is visible. To the left is the old harbour with the city and the mountains behind. One may wander at leisure through the old streets of the citadel, where Victor Hugo lived as a child.

The route back into town is along a left fork of the Cours Dr Favale called the Boulevard Auguste Gaudin, which goes down to the Place Moro Giafferi. On the left is the nineteenth century ⌘ **Palais de Justice**, where the inner courtyard has columns of bluish marble from the area around Corte.

Leading off to the right is Bastia's chief thoroughfare, the Boulevard Paoli. This road bends and then forks, the left fork being the Rue César Campinchi, which runs parallel to it as far as the Avenue Maréchal Sébastiani. It passes the theatre on the left. The left wing of the theatre also houses the city library, which possesses several very valuable tomes.

A road to the right leads back down to the old harbour. To the left off the Quai de la Santé is a flight of steps leading up to the

The Old Quarter, Bastia

cathedral of **St John the Baptist**, which is set back from the ⌘
harbour. It was founded in 1640; in the eighteenth century the
Baroque façade was added and the interior was refurbished. The
central altar is made of multicoloured Corsican marble.

If one turns left out of the cathedral, one quickly comes into
the Place de l'Hôtel de Ville, with the town hall on the left and a
Protestant church on the right. There is a market here in the
morning — an everyday local event which is of great interest to
visitors. This square forms the centre of the oldest part of the
town — the Terra Vecchia.

A left turn past the town hall along the Rue Neuve brings one
into the Rue Napoléon, which runs parallel to the Boulevard Paoli.
There are two more chapels here: to the left the **Chapelle de
l'Immaculée Conception** (1590), and to the right the **Chapelle de St Roch** (1604). The former contains a genuine Murillo
altar piece, the latter a statue of St Roch in multicoloured marble.
The Rue Napoléon goes into the Place St Nicolas, at the other end
of which is the Avenue Maréchal Sébastiani.

Just north of the new harbour is the town's main bathing area
— a shingly beach called the Plage de Toga, which is often very
crowded. There are many more bathing beaches nearby, both to
the north along the rocky coast of Cap Corse, and to the south
along the spit that runs in front of the Etang de Biguglia.

There are two interesting old forts on the adjoining slopes
called **Fort Lacroix** and **Fort Straforello**. These, together
with **St Anthony's Convent**, are within easy walking distance
from the town. The shorter route goes up past the Palais de
Justice; the longer one takes about an hour, and involves a right
turn opposite the entrance to the citadel.

Two other local places of interest are the tiny **Chapelle de
Ste Lucie**, on the D31 to Pietrabugno (5km) from by the station;
and the old village of **Cardo** (350m), which is served by an hourly
bus service from the Boulevard Paoli. Both provide magnificent
views of the area and across to Italy.

Excursions from Bastia

Short Tour of Cap Corse (24km)
Following the D31 northwards through the mountains via Pietrabugno and San Martino-di-Lota to Miomo on the coast, returning
along the coast. (For the longer tour see **Cap Corse** .)

La Canonica, Mariana

Short Tour of Nebbio (41km)
Via the **Col de Teghime** (10km; see route 2) and the **Défilé de Lancone** (15km from Bastia). See **Nebbio** .

Longer Tour of Nebbio (63km)
Via **St Florent** (23km; see route 2) and **Murato** (23km from Bastia). See **Nebbio** .

Mariana and La Canonica (23km)
17km south of Bastia along the N193 (see route 3), there is a right turn for Poretta Airport. The area to the south of the airport is full of interesting things to see.

Visitors without private transport are recommended to take the airport bus from the railway station in Bastia, and to continue on foot from the airport (20 minutes). It is a further 3km to the nearby beach, from which car drivers may return to Bastia along the spit that runs in front of the Etang de Biguglia.

Mariana was originally founded in AD 93, when a Roman commander called Marius founded a settlement near the mouth of the River Golo. Little has been found from the Roman period, as the settlement was several times destroyed by enemies or floods.

The present 'village' consists of three houses only! The chief area of archaeological interest is just north of here and immediately next to the church of La Canonica. Discoveries have included the foundations of an early Christian church with a baptistry from the fourth century AD. It was extended in the fifth and tenth centuries, and reveals some fascinating mosaics.

La Canonica itself is more correctly named the Basilica of St ⌘ Mary of Mariana. The original marble-faced building was built in the early twelfth century around the remains of a ninth-century structure, and was consecrated in 1120. It was destroyed by the Saracens in the sixteenth century, but has more recently been rebuilt, and was reconsecrated in 1931.

It is thought to have been the prototype for other Pisan churches on Corsica. The narrow central nave is 13m high, and is divided by square pillars from the 8m high nave-aisles. The whole building is 32m long and 12m wide. There are three windows in the apse at the east end, which, like the roof arches, is decorated with friezes. The entrance arch has some beautiful frescos, depicting among others a pack of hounds chasing a deer, several griffins and a lamb. Above the arch are a window and a cross. The pilasters inside are reminiscent of the Renaissance, and reveal some interesting Doric designs; elsewhere there are unmistakably Gothic features.

The restoration has been kept as simple as possible, but is not yet quite finished. However, services are regularly held here. At one time the church was used as a cathedral, and was the seat of Corsica's first bishop and chapter.

About 500m away, and directly by the 'village', is another old ⌘ Romanesque church. San Parteo is very similar to St Mary's, but smaller and simpler in design. The white marble columns in the apse have Corinthian capitals, which probably came from the nearby Roman remains. The frieze over the side entrance reveals an oriental design, showing a tree with an animal either side.

Nearby on the banks of the Golo are the remains of the old Roman bridge and baths. It will be a long time before more can be known of the Roman town, which has been covered by many centuries of silt.

⌘ **Aléria** (70km; see route 3)

The modern village of Aléria (population 800) is situated on a rocky knoll just south of the River Tavignano. It was founded in the thirteenth century, and later became important as a bishopric. Then in the fifteenth century the Genoese built Fort Matra to defend it.

The original site, however, was one of the oldest settlements on Corsica. It was founded in 564 BC by Greeks from Phocaea. They called their town Alalia, and it later became quite a prosperous port. The Romans destroyed it in 259 BC during the first of the Punic Wars, but a small settlement remained. Then in 81 BC the Romans founded a large military colony here, using the nearby lagoon as an anchoring place for their fleet. They called it Aléria, and it soon grew in population to between 20,000 and 30,000. In AD 450 the town received a battering from the Vandals, and in the ninth century it was totally destroyed by the Saracens.

For centuries the Roman ruins lay hidden under layers of mud and silt. The drainage channels disappeared, and the whole area became a malarial swamp that was singularly unsuitable for habitation. Not until the 1950s were attempts made to reclaim the land for agriculture. Archaeologists had already begun to excavate the site in the 1920s, but their work is still far from finished and will take decades to complete.

Fort Matra has been turned into a small museum, which provides vivid insights into the life of the old Roman town. Maps and sketches help to explain the significance of the plentiful archaeological evidence. The site has yielded examples of Greek and Roman art that have astounded specialists both here and elsewhere. And museums outside Corsica would be willing to pay any price for some of the treasures that have been found here.

Next to the fort is St Mark's Church. This was built in 1462 on the site of the old cathedral, which in turn rested on the foundations of a fourth-century structure.

A small path goes to the left of the fort to the part of the Roman town that has already been excavated. It is an opportunity to step back into the past; for with a little imagination it is possible to picture the old Roman town on the hill overlooking the surrounding plains.

In the middle of the site are the remains of an old archway. This was the first thing to be discovered, and goes back to the earliest days of the Roman town. In those days it formed the eastern entrance to the governor's praetorium on the edge of the forum.

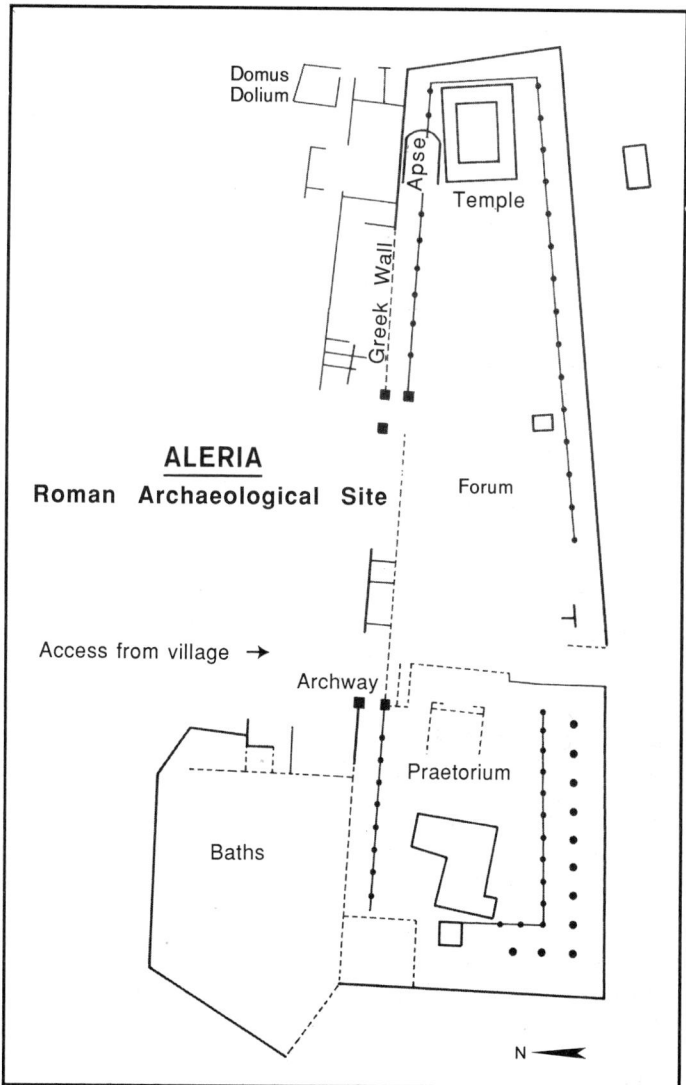

Domus
Dolium

Apse

Greek Wall

Temple

ALERIA
Roman   Archaeological   Site

Forum

Access from village →

Archway

Praetorium

Baths

N ◄━

The forum itself is 92m long and trapezoid in plan; it occupies
the middle part of the site. The columns were built out of bricks
and covered with rendering. The praetorium stood at the western

The Roman site of Aléria

end of the forum. To the north of the praetorium was the bath-house, where several mosaic floors and cisterns have been uncovered and are on view to the public.

At the eastern end of the forum, the foundations of the temple are still visible. On the north side of the temple, superimposed over a row of column stumps, are the foundations of the apse of an early Christian church. To the north of this are the foundations of a house known as the Domus Dolium, where yet more floor mosaics have been found.

The northern row of columns appears to have extended onto higher ground further east, where a number of Greek remains have been found. This was presumably an acropolis, and the main part of the town must have covered both the present site and the strip of low-lying land between the acropolis and the river. The port was located here in an area now to the east of the main N198 road, where the remains of a second- or third-century bath-house have been uncovered. These are known as the Thermes de Santa Laurina.

The centuries-old mud of Aléria will no doubt reveal yet more secrets in the future as archaeologists continue to dig.

Further Excursions

Cap Corse Peninsula

The peninsula of Cap Corse is the most northerly part of the island. It is about 40km long and about 15km wide, and is in many ways a microcosm of the whole island. A range of mountains forms the backbone of the peninsula, the highest point being Monte Stello at 1,305m. The west coast is extremely steep and rocky, while the east coast is somewhat gentler. Both sides have a good sprinkling of beaches in small sandy coves.

The people live mostly from wine-growing and market gardening, and the majority live up in the valleys. The villages are linked to little ports (*marines*) on the coast, where a small amount of fishing is carried on.

There is now a good road all round the peninsula. The D80 follows the coast closely on the east and west sides of the cape, while at the northern end it goes overland for a short distance. 10km further south, the D180 provides a short cut overland, saving about 21km. The only other crossing apart from the D81 over the **Col de Teghime** (see route 2) is the D35, which is partly unmade.

A round trip of the peninsula via the D80 coast road and the Col de Teghime is about 120km long altogether. The distance can be covered in 3 hours, but visitors are advised to allow a whole day so as to include sightseeing stops.

It is a good idea to leave **Bastia** early in the morning so as to get the full benefit of the daylight. The route goes north via **Pietranera** (2½km) to **Miomo** (another 3km). There is an alternative route to Miomo through the mountains, which is 13km longer (see page 97). Miomo has a small shingle beach with a Genoese watchtower overlooking it.

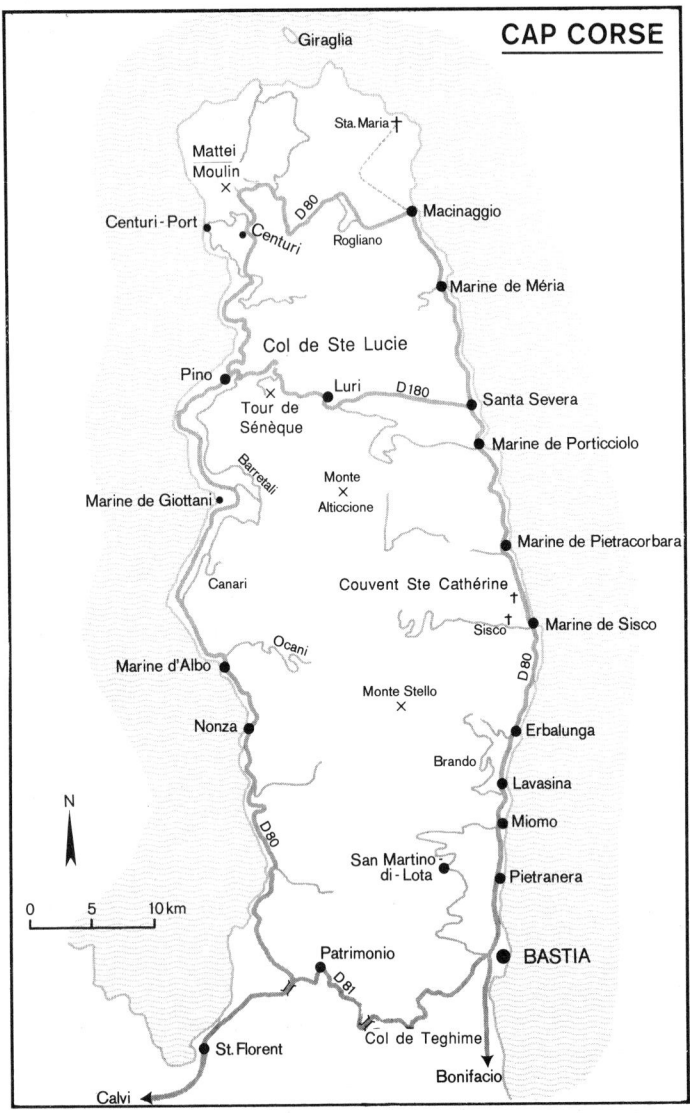

CAP CORSE

Giraglia

Sta. Maria †

Mattei
Moulin
×

Centuri-Port

Centuri

D80

Rogliano

Macinaggio

Marine de Méria

Col de Ste Lucie

Pino

Luri   D180

Santa Severa

Tour de
Sénèque

Marine de Porticciolo

Barretali

Monte
×
Alticcione

Marine de Giottani

Marine de Pietracorbara

Canari

Couvent Ste Cathérine
†

Ocani

Sisco

Marine de Sisco

Marine d'Albo

D80

Monte Stello
×

Nonza

Erbalunga

Brando

Lavasina

N

Miomo

San Martino
di-Lota

Pietranera

D80

0   5   10 km

Patrimonio

BASTIA

D81

Col de Teghime

St. Florent

Bonifacio

Calvi

⌘   2km further north at **Lavasina** there is an interesting
seventeenth-century church. Above its black-and-white marble
altar is a painting of the Madonna, which is supposed to have

miraculous properties. The bell tower is separate, and is topped by rather ugly concrete statue of the holy mother and child.

Lavasina belongs to the parish of **Brando** — a group of small hamlets inland from the coast. The D54 runs through them to form a loop road between Lavasina and Erbalunga (see below). 2¹/2km before Erbalunga is **Castello**, where the ruins of an old castle can be seen to the left. It belonged to the Gentile family, the former owners of southern Cap Corse. To the right is a small Romanesque chapel, which is rather oddly named Notre Dame des Neiges or 'Our Lady of the Snows'. Built in the thirteenth century, it has a timbered ceiling and a number of fourteenth-century frescos.

Just after Castello there is a turning for **Silgaggia** at the foot of **Monte Stello** (1,305m) — the highest peak on Cap Corse. The summit is two to three hours' climb away.

The D80 runs directly along the coast from Lavasina to Erbalunga (2¹/2km). About 1km before Erbalunga, there is a footpath to the left leading up to the Brando Grotto. It is about twenty-five minutes walk away and is closed to visitors, but there is a wonderful view from in front of it.

Erbalunga itself is probably the best-known place on the eastern side of the cape. This dreamy little spot was once the exclusive domain of artists and romantics. But the old village is now ringed by hotels and shops, and tourists come in droves to savour its old-world charms.

The old part has fortunately lost none of its charm. It clings to a rocky promontory around a large round watchtower, noted for the large breach in its walls. Visitors may stroll through the narrow streets past the slate-covered houses of the well-to-do and the more modest dwellings of the simple folk.

A ruined church by the square is the site for a *son et lumière* performance which is staged every year on Napoléon's birthday. The modern church on the coast road has no tower. The atmosphere is further enhanced by the fishermen plying their modest trade on the waters of the tiny harbour.

There is another viewing point at Brando Abbey on the valley slopes to the north of Erbalunga. This old Benedictine monastery is now privately owned and has been turned into a guesthouse.

The coast road continues along a twisty section high above the shore to **Marine de Sisco**. This is the port belonging to **Sisco** — a scattered parish of small hamlets distributed along the D32 road that runs up the valley. There are two small

⌘ churches worth visiting. St Michael's is Romanesque and has an interesting frieze, while St Martin's contains some valuable relics.

Sisco was once a very rich parish; right up to the eighteenth century, its people were renowned for their skill as weavers and smiths. One of the best examples is in St Martin's Church itself. It is the copper mask of St John Chrysostom, which is covered with hand-forged gold and silver designs.

Beneath the main altar is a wooden sanctuary. There are only three keys to open it; these are in the possession of three different curators, and they lock them in separate boxes, which they keep hidden in the church. The sanctuary is supposed to contain some of the oldest relics in the world, including almonds from the Garden of Eden, a small piece of the soil from which God created the first man, the rod used by Moses when he parted the waters of the Red Sea, and of course the actual rod of Aaron! They were originally kept at the nearby Ste Cathérine's Convent, but in about 1580 they were moved inland to Sisco, where they were thought to be safer.

⌘ Ste Cathérine's Convent is about 1km north of Marine de Sisco, and overlooks the coast road to the left. In front of it is a statue of Ste Cathérine, the patron saint of fishermen. A nearby grotto is also named after her. The fifteenth-century church is very simple in plan. The frescos on the façade are particularly beautiful, and are partly turned inwards. The pulpit looks out onto the outside as well as the inside of the church.

The structure is built over a twelfth-century crypt known as *il tombolo*, which is hewn out of the bare rock. It is thought to have been a copy of the Holy Sepulchre in Jerusalem, and was the original home of the relics which are now kept at St Martin's Church (see above). According to legend, the relics arrived here by accident. During the Middle Ages there was a very lucrative trade in relics; a ship is supposed to have got into difficulties in a storm off Cap Corse, and the captain swore that if he survived the ordeal he would give the relics he had on board to the nearest church he could find.

Returning to the present, the route continues for another 3km along the coast road past a cement factory to the beautiful beach of **Marine de Pietracorbara**, which is overlooked by a ruined tower. This again belongs to a scattered parish made up of hamlets along the road up the valley. From the top end of the valley there is a path to the summit of **Monte Alticcione** (1,138m), but it is very difficult and suitable only for expert climbers.

Pino

On the approach to **Marine de Porticciolo** (5km) the road
passes a particularly well-preserved tower called the Tour de
Losse. The port itself is rather larger than some of the others
along the coast, but still belongs to the scattered inland parish of
Cagnano. There is a marvellous sandy beach to the north of the
village.

It is another 2km to **Santa Severa**. Visitors who are in a
hurry, or who are tired of the twists and turns along the coast road
(there are more of these to follow), may care to take a short cut
along the D180 through the fertile valley of the Luri to Pino/Ciocce
on the west coast of the cape (16km).

The road is fairly straight and gentle for the first 5km as far as
Piazza (112m), the main village in the parish of **Luri.** At first it
runs past fields of grazing sheep and copses of cork oaks. But
the vegetation soon becomes more luxuriant, with maize, vines
and a whole variety of fruit trees including citron, orange, almond,
walnut, olive and fig.

After Poggio there is a steep climb up the **Col de Ste Lucie**

(380m). The road plunges through thick forests, and the mountains become closer. High above the road is a Genoese tower called the Tour de Sénèque ('Seneca's Tower') after the Roman philosopher of that name, who is supposed to have lived there in exile between 49 and 43 BC. The hills behind soon resemble the waves of the sea. The pass itself has been eroded into a narrow defile. There is a chapel dedicated to Ste Lucie, and a path up to Seneca's Tower, from which there is a magnificent view. To the east one can gaze across pine forests, down the valley to the sea, and beyond to the island of Elba. To the west there are no trees to hide the road as it winds down the almost vertical slope to Pino/Ciocce (5km) — a route that commands respect if not fear (see page 111).

The east-coast route continues northwards from **Santa Severa** for a good 6km to the small harbour that belongs to the inland village of **Méria**. On the opposite side of the valley is another old watchtower.

It is another 4km to **Macinaggio,** whose lighthouse can be seen from some distance away. Macinaggio today is a popular sailing resort, but it also has strong links with the past. In 1767 Paoli's forces embarked from here to conquer the islands of Giraglia to the north of Cap Corse. When Paoli returned from exile in 1790, it was at Macinaggio that he first stepped on Corsican soil. Only 3 years later Napoléon landed here, and in 1869 the Empress Eugénie arrived here on her return from a trip to the Far East. It is difficult to imagine these events when one looks at the harbour today.

There is a nice beach to the north, which is 20 minutes' walk over almost pathless coastal terrain. Walkers are recommended to continue along the coast for another 20 minutes until they are level with the offshore islands of Finocchiarola. There is another small beach here in a rocky cove. Nearby are an old watchtower and the lovely little church of Sta Maria della Chiapella. The latter was restored in the eighteenth century, and is a popular destination for pilgrims and artistically-minded tourists. With its twin apses, it is typical of Pisan churches on Corsica. There is also an interesting menhir not far away.

Macinaggio is the port for the eight hamlets that make up the parish of **Rogliano**, and that overlook the D80 road as it crosses overland to the west coast. The D53 makes a 13km detour through them, coming back into the D80 5¹/₂km from Macinaggio. The D53 runs through some beautiful scenery past an old

Centuri, famous for its lobster catch

monastery and numerous ruined towers and castles. Rogliano
was the home of the Da Mare family, the one-time owners of
northern Cap Corse.

A vast, ugly dome becomes visible among the mountains to

the south, and keeps coming into view along the next part of the
route as far as Pino and beyond. It is in fact an observatory in the
middle of the nearby military zone.

The road climbs over the **Col de St Nicolas** (300m) and
down to **Ersa** (4km). At Ersa there are two small roads leading off
up to the northern coast of the cape and the tiny village of
Barcaggio, which is Corsica's most northerly settlement.

But the best view of the cape is still to come as the road climbs
up the **Col de Serra** (369m). From here it is only 5 minutes' walk
to the Moulin Mattei (389m) — a windmill on the top of a hill with a
magnificent view.

Windmills were once plentiful on Corsica, and were used for
grinding corn and olive stones. Most of them have now fallen into
disrepair, but a few of them are used for alternative purposes.
This one, for instance, has been transformed by the famous
Mattei wine firm into an advertisement for its wine and its citron
liqueur (*cédratine*). The trade mark — an outline of Corsica — has
been painted on the front of the mill, and the terrace around has
been converted into an attractive hostelry with stone tables and
benches.

There is a view to the north across the northern tip of Cap
Corse, while the west coast of the peninsula stretches out to the
south. Villages cling to the steep, rocky slopes beneath tall
churches and watchtowers, with the road running in a thin band
between them and a long line of mountains behind. One can see
way beyond them to the Gulf of St Florent, the hills of the Désert
des Agriates and the rest of northern Corsica.

The D80 now turns sharply southwards. 2km after the Col de
Serra is the tiny village of **Camera** — one of a cluster of lovely
little villages that together form the parish of **Centuri**. The
church is on the opposite side of the road from the village. There
is a turning here along the D35 loop road via the coast, which
comes back into the main road at Pruno. A small side-road goes
off to **Cannelle** — the most northerly village in the parish,
directly below the Moulin Mattei.

Down by the sea is **Centuri-Port** — a small cluster of green-
roofed houses, with three churches and an old tower. It is famous
for its lobsters, which the fishermen bring in between nine and ten
o'clock every morning. On a rock out to sea are the remains of an
old chapel.

Pruno is 2km south of Camera along the D80. It is the main
village in the parish of Morsiglia, and clings high up on a steep

rocky slope above the sea. Several old watchtowers can be seen along the coast. At the top of a hill to the left is the Chapel of the Madonna (542m), which is all that remains of an old monastery.

The 10km to Pino are along a particularly beautiful stretch of coastline. The D80 goes round a headland called **Capo Corvoli**, and there is a lovely view across the Gulf of Aliso to Pino, which extends up the hillside from sea level up to height of 400m. The road continues at a height of about 145m above the shore, and provides a foretaste of what is to come. For the coast of Cap Corse is much steeper on the west than the east; the road winds interminably as it descends into the gullies where the streams come down and then climbs up to the villages again. The terrain alternates between sheer cliffs and *maquis*-covered slopes or terraces with orchards and vineyards.

Just before Pino there is a turning along the D180, which first winds steeply over the **Col de Ste Lucie**, and then continues to Santa Severa on the east coast. There is a magnificent view from the top of the pass (5km).

Pino/Ciocce straddles the hillside between the road and the shore, and is set amid a forest of chestnut and plane trees, full of vines and climbing flowers. It is overlooked by the free-standing bell tower of the Baroque church. Just below the main road is an old square keep, and there is a ruined watchtower on a rock down by the shore. In between the two is a fifteenth-century Franciscan monastery, which is now used as a boarding school.

Just after Pino there is a turning onto the D33, which runs parallel to the coast road but much higher up the mountainside. It passes through a series of small villages belonging to the parishes of Barretali and Canari (see below), and re-enters the D80 near Abro. Though the views are dramatic, it is not a road for the faint-hearted. It is very hard work for the driver, as there is only a tiny parapet to prevent the car from plunging down over the precipice; but it can be great fun for the passengers!

Most drivers prefer to stay on the coast road, which continues from Pino around the **Punta Minervio** (3km) to **Minerbio** (another 2km). Just before Minerbio, the road passes Corsica's most famous mausoleum. It is a kind of pavilion with a colonnade, a dome and a statue of Mary on top, which must have cost millions!

The road loops inland as it passes the next bay so as to cross the small river that comes in here. It passes **Marine de Giottani** on the shore to the right, and the hamlets belonging to

Barretali on the mountainside to the left. 9km from Minerbio the road goes through **Marinca** — the westernmost hamlet in the parish of **Canari**, which is famous for its wine.

4km further on the road runs through an area covered in white asbestos dust. The only plants are a few rather pathetic fig cactuses, which nonetheless make valiant attempts to blossom and produce fruit. The rocky mountains on the left climb to about 1,000m. About 600m up the mountainside is the disused shell of a factory, which was once the largest asbestos works in the whole of Europe, and the only one in France. It was closed in 1968 because the high cost of transport (overland to Bastia and then by ship) made it uneconomic. The environmental damage seems even more dramatic when viewed from the south — a white scar that runs down the hillside right down to the sea.

2km further on is **Marine d'Albo**, where coaches often stop for a longer break. There is a good restaurant, together with a number of small hotels, and a 5km long sandy beach extends from here to Nonza. The sand is black-coloured from the particles of slate in it, and there is a bar of rock dividing it from the clear blue-green waters of the sea. There is a well-preserved watchtower on the left by the stream, which usually dries up in the summer. The hillside is covered with a dense layer of *maquis*.

At the entrance to **Nonza** is the sixteenth-century church of Sta Julia. Inside is a marble altar with a beautifully worked centrepiece, and behind it a painting of the saint herself. A steep path goes down to a spring known as the **Fontaine des Mamelles** ('Fountain of the Breasts') or the Fontaine de Ste Julie. Both names hark back to the legend of the martyrdom of Sta Julia, in which her breasts were cut off and a fountain sprang up where they fell. Some authorities suggest that it actually took place here, while others merely attribute this association to the fact that the church was dedicated to her. The ruined chapel nearby is supposed to have been destroyed by the Saracens in AD 734.

From the roadside there is a view back along the black sandy beach, with the asbestos works in the background. There is also a good view of Nonza itself, which is crowned by a massive square keep on a rock that rises 152m almost sheer from the sea. Of the four white domes, only three still remain. This was the site of an interesting and rather amusing historical event.

It happened in 1768 during the French campaign against Paoli's independent state. The French arrived at Nonza to find gun barrels aimed at them from all the loopholes in the keep, and estimated a garrison of at least 200 soldiers. They offered terms, which were eventually accepted on condition that the garrison was allowed to retreat with full military honours. One can imagine their astonishment when only a single man emerged from the keep!

The village is a sight to behold. The houses cling to the rock, surrounded by chestnut and plane trees and covered with flowers. One can climb up to the keep and enjoy the fresh sea breezes and the view. On a clear day one can see as far as Calvi. 2km further south is an old ruined monastery, which clings to the hillside just below the road, overlooked by the shell of the church tower. Further up the hillside is another mausoleum.

Only 8km further on, the road turns inland and leaves the beauties of the coast behind. One is reluctant to leave the small hamlets and coves either side of the road, and the last of the twenty watchtowers that line the shore of Cap Corse. For those coming in the opposite direction, the view provides a marvellous foretaste of the drama and beauty to come. Many drivers may prefer to do the journey that way round, since they will then be driving on the upslope side of the road!

There is a final glimpse of the sea before the **Col de San Bernardino** (76m), where the road comes into the D81. To the right it is only 5km to St Florent, while to the left it is 18km over the Col de Teghime to Bastia (see route 2).

The Nebbio Region

Nebbio is the region adjoining Cap Corse to the south. It lies south of the D81 road from St Florent to Bastia (see route 2), and west of the N193 road south of Bastia (see route 3).

It is a very pretty area, and though hilly is very fertile, producing fruit and vegetables, wine, olives and mulberry leaves for silkworms. Numerous small villages cling to the hillsides amid groves of chestnut trees. It is full of small rivers that run down to the sea, the most important being the Aliso, which caused the harbour at St Florent to silt up. Nebbio has much to offer visitors, from beautiful scenery to Pisan churches and prehistoric remains.

The suggested route goes from Bastia southwards along the N193, then after 9km turns right along the D82 for the Col de San Stefano (9km) and St Florent (22km). After about 1km, the road

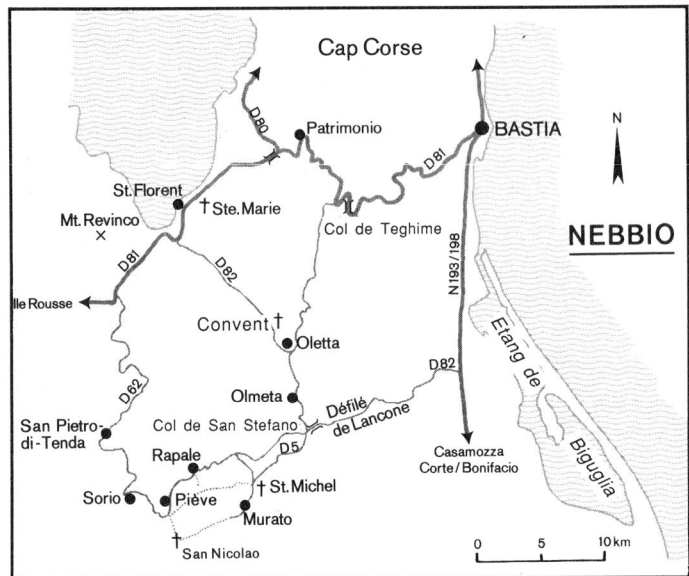

leaves the flat coastal plain and begins to climb. From the Col de St Antoine (66m) there is a view back across the plain to the sea.

About 5km further on, at a height of 282m, the road becomes narrow as it runs across the hillside above a deep gorge called the **Défilé de Lancone**, with the River Bevinco at the bottom. The daylight produces a beautiful variegated pattern on the bare rocks of the gorge.

After about 1½km the valley broadens out again, and the road soon arrives at the **Col de San Stefano** (349m), where it turns sharply to the right. Those following the short Nebbio route should continue along the D82 to Oletta (see page 116), and turn right there for the Col de Teghime.

If possible, however, the longer route is very much more interesting. For this one should take the D5 for Murato, which is the middle of three left turns from the top of the pass. It continues to climb up the hillside to **Murato** (497m).

About 1km before Murato the road comes to the beautiful Pisan church of St Michel, also known as San Michele. Built in the thirteenth century, it is square in plan like San Parteo at Mariana. The bell tower is supported by two columns which form a porch in front of the entrance. It is built of a mixture of limestone and slate, which combine nicely to give the church an air of lightness and elegance. Above the entrance, two marble peacocks are mounted on the limestone door lintel. There are one or two other small sculptures remaining. Of the interior frescos only one has been preserved, but this is one of the best of its kind. To appreciate the exterior, one should view the church from a point higher up. From the churchyard there is a magnificent view across to the Gulf of St Florent.

There is a road junction near the church, from which a link road (2km) goes north to join the D62 from the Col de San Stefano to San Pietro-di-Tenda and Murato (32¹/₂km). Turning left here, one soon comes to **Rapale** (2km). Half an hour's walk to the south of Rapale is the Romanesque chapel of San Cesareo, which can also be reached on foot via a path from St Michel de Murato. Like St Michel, it is built of a mixture of limestone and slate, but it is in a considerable state of disrepair.

2¹/₂km further along the D62, and just over a pass (427m), is the village of **Piève**, where two menhirs from the area have been placed in front of the church. They are known as Bucentone and Murello. The path from St Michel via San Cesareo also comes out at Piève. Another path runs southward to yet another Roman-esque chapel called San Nicolao, and eventually comes out into the D5, 2km above Murato.

The D62 continues to **Sorio** (2km). South-west of the village is the third Romanesque chapel in the area; called Sta Marguerita, it too has fallen into disrepair. 7km to the south-west, the ruined octagonal baptistry of **San Giacomo** can be easily seen in its dominating position at the top of the Col de Tenda (1,219m). It can be reached via a path that goes over the pass.

The road goes on for another 5¹/₂km via San Gavino-di-Tenda to **San Pietro-di-Tenda** (362m), which has a church built of reddish stone with a separate bell tower. Nine menhirs have been found on the nearby Capo Castinco. They include a head which once belonged to a 3m high stone statue, known in Corsican as *u Frate* ('the brother'). Like the other menhirs found in northern Corsica, they have been attributed to the last phase of the early Megalithic culture. It has not yet been decided where these menhirs are eventually to be exhibited.

Immediately after San Pietro-di-Tenda, the road passes the ruins of a Franciscan monastery. 11km further on the D62 comes into the main D81 road from Calvi to Bastia (see route 2). To the

Gulf of St Florent

left are the hills of the Désert des Agriates, while to the right it is only 5km to St Florent. North of the road, and about half-way to the Fornali lighthouse on the coast, is Monte Revinco, at the foot of which four dolmens were discovered, including the famous Casa dell' Orcu.

St Florent is situated on a peninsula that juts out into the bay. On a hill above it is the Pisan basilica of Ste Marie de Nebbio, which is made of marble from Táranto. Both places should be included in any visitor's itinerary (see route 2).

The present route turns right before St Florent, and returns along the D82 to the Col de San Stefano (see above). The road runs along a river valley as far as Oletta. About 1km before the village, it passes the old monastery of St François on the left.

Oletta nestles among the terraces on the hillside. It is the richest village in Nebbio, thanks to the rearing of silkworms and to the stone from a nearby quarry. The beautiful setting and the plentiful footpaths make it an ideal retreat for the visitor who wants to get away from it all. The church contains a lovely sixteenth-century triptych and a picture of the Madonna which is supposed to have miraculous powers. The façade includes a bas-relief that originally came from the previous church on the site. A small road to the left climbs up to join the D81 on the Col de

Teghime (9km; see route 2).

On the way to the Col de San Stefano (4km), the road passes Olmeta-di-Tuda and the castle of Marshal Sébastiani. When it arrives at the top of the pass, this completes the circular tour of the region of Nebbio.

The Castagniccia Region

The name Castagniccia means 'chestnut forest' — an apt description for this region of medium-sized mountains in north-eastern Corsica, where every valley slope is covered with forests of chestnut trees. The effect is most dramatic in the late autumn, when the leaves turn golden-brown. The sweet chestnut is a staple food on Corsica, for both humans and animals alike. Some of the chestnut crop is left over for export.

Before the industrial revolution the region was relatively wealthy, thanks to the local agriculture and artisan industries. Since then it has become depopulated like much of the rest of the

CASTAGNICCIA

Bastia
Poretta Airport
Mariana
Casamozza
N198
Barchetta
N193
Vescovato
Venzolasca
Loreto
Ile Rousse
Ponte Nuovo
Silvareccio
D506
Folelli
Castello-
di-Rostino
N193
Ponte Leccia
Source de Caldane
D71
La Porta
Corte
Morosaglia
Monte
San Pietro
Couvent d'Orezza
San
Nicolao
Moriani-Plage
Piedicroce
Eaux d'Orezza
N
Carcheto
Ste.
Christine
Cervione
Prunete-
Cervione
0   5   10 km
Valle d'Alesani
D71
Couvent d'Alesani
Aleria

island, though it is still relatively densely populated by Corsican standards. Most of the villages are prettily situated on the tops of hills at altitudes of between 500m and 700m. Some of them have been turned into popular mountain resorts, both for resident guests and for day-trippers from the coast.

The suggested tour begins in the north-east of the region in the area known as **Casinca**. 2km south of **Casamozza**, there is a right turn off the N198 (see route 3) along the D237, which after 3km arrives at the lovely village of **Vescovato** (167m). Three of the island's greatest heroes were born here in the fifteenth and sixteenth centuries.

The first part of the route is from Vescovato to Piedicroce in the heart of Castagniccia (26km). From near **Venzolasca** (3km) there is a lovely view across the coastal plain, and also of **Loreto-di-Casinca**, to which a side-road goes off (2¹⁄₂km). 2¹⁄₂km further along the D237, there is a turning for **Castellare-di-Casinca** and the coast road.

The D237 climbs over the Col de San Agostino and arrives at **Silvareccio** (6km). The route goes left here along a link road via **Casalta** and enters the D506, which runs along the valley of the Fium' Alto. 12km to the east is Folelli on the coast road (see route 3), while Piedicroce is 10km up the valley to the south-west. 3km to the east of the road junction is a ferruginous (iron-bearing) spring called the Source de Caldane.

About 3km before Piedicroce there is a turning for the **Eaux d'Orezza** — the most important mineral springs on the whole of Corsica. They are highly ferruginous, and are used for the treatment of anaemia and for disorders of the liver and digestion. They serve the tiny spa resort of **Stazzona** between here and Piedicroce.

Piedicroce is the regional centre of Castagniccia, and is situated on the D71 about half-way between Prunete on the coast and Ponte Leccia on the N193 Ajaccio-Bastia road (see route 5). The village's only building of interest is the Baroque church of St Peter and St Paul. But there is more to be seen in the surrounding hamlets that cling to terraces on the wooded hillsides above the Fium' Alto spa region.

One place of special interest is **Campodonico** (636m), which can be reached via a narrow road that comes off the D71 about 1km north of Piedicroce (towards Ponte Leccia). It lies at the foot of a bare rocky summit about half an hour's climb away. The small church is remarkable for its bell tower, which consists of four tree-trunks supporting a corrugated iron roof. Near to the road junction for Campodonico are the ruins of the historic Couvent d'Orezza, where the Corsican freedom-fighters formally rescinded their oath of loyalty to Genoa in 1731.

The next part of the route goes south-east from Piedicroce along the D71 towards Cervione. The 18km section to Valle d'Alesani is particularly beautiful. The road winds past Pie-d'Orezza and Piedipartino, and passes a small waterfall on the left. The church at **Carcheto** contains a beautifully simple representation of the Stations of the Cross.

The road climbs over the **Col d'Arcarotta** (820m), from which there is a lovely view across the hills to Monte San Petrone (1,767m). It is another 9km to Querceto, which forms the focal point of the scattered hamlets that make up the parish of **Valle d'Alesani**.

At the next hamlet of Castagneto there is a right turn for Piazzali. Just outside Piazzali is the famous abbey of St François d'Alesani — one of many in Castagniccia that gave assistance to the Corsican freedom-fighters. It was here that a constitution was drafted for an independent Corsica, and that the German Baron von Neuhoff was crowned king of Corsica in 1736. The abbey contains a fifteenth-century Madonna known as *La Vierge à la Cérise* ('The Cherry Virgin'), and some of the most beautiful sculptures on the island.

The D71 continues to twist and turn as it runs along the valley of the Alesani. After about 12km it swings north for the last 4km to **Cervione** (326m). Cervione has a population of 1,400, and enjoys a commanding position on the eastern flank of the Castagniccia mountains. It is surrounded by vineyards and groves of chestnut and olive trees. 7km to the east, the D71 enters the coast road near Prunete (see route 3). The summit of Monte Castello (1,107) rises up to the west.

The king of Corsica resided here during his brief reign in the former bishop's palace (the bishops of Aléria had transferred to Cervione in the sixteenth century). Opposite the bishop's palace is the sixteenth-century domed cathedral of St Mary and St Erasmus, which includes among its treasures a beautifully carved bishop's throne.

Just outside Cervione is St Christine's Church, famous for its twin apses and well-preserved frescos. Built in the fifteenth century, it is situated at the end of a footpath about 1km to the north of the hamlet of Valle-di-Campoloro, where a key can be obtained from the priest.

There is another path to the south-west of Cervione leading to a lookout point known as the Belvédère de Cervione (805m). It takes about an hour to get there. The path goes past the chapel of Notre Dame de la Scobiccia, where a sixteenth-century white marble statue is supposed to have come from a ship that was wrecked on the coast.

The route turns north from Cervione along the D330 to **San Nicolao**, which again is charmingly situated on the edge of the mountains. Its population is supposed to be the same as its height in metres above sea level (250). If one stops by a small waterfall just south of the village, there is a beautiful view across the sea to the tiny Italian island of Montecristo. The Baroque church is on a hill to the north of the village, and is dominated by its separate bell tower. It was built to replace the original Romanesque building, a few remnants of which can still be seen.

The route leaves San Nicolao along the D34, which after 5km comes into the N198 coast road at Moriani-Plage (see route 3).

8 CALVI

Holiday Centre in the North-West

Calvi in north-western Corsica was originally a Roman settlement which fell victim to the attacks of the Vandals and Goths, and was eventually destroyed by the Saracens. It was refounded by the Genoese in the thirteenth century, who built it, not at the foot of the bare, rocky headland, as the Romans had done, but right on top of it. They called it Calvi from the word *calvo*, meaning 'bald', and the Genoese citadel still dominates the bay.

Calvi was unsuitable as a port because the sea was too shallow here, but it was an ideal site for a military garrison. Its inhabitants, like those of Bonifacio, were granted special status as a guarantee of their loyalty. The Genoese rewarded Calvi with the title *semper fidelis* ('ever faithful'). Indeed, the city remained faithful to Genoa to the last, and then became faithful to France. It was off Calvi that the British Admiral Nelson received the shot that cost him an eye (a plaque marks the spot where it was fired from). For this the French re-affirmed the title of *semper fidelis*, which Calvi bears proudly in its coat of arms to this day.

Calvi today has a population of 3,500. It no longer lives primarily from fishing (especially lobsters) and agriculture, but from the tourist industry. It is busiest in the high summer, when the tourists flock to its broad, shallow beach, lined by pine trees. In winter the town seems to go into hibernation, but it suddenly bursts into life with the approach of the tourist season. The hotels are full, and the tents vie for space beneath the shade of the stone pines. The car- and boat-hire firms, and coach and minibus operators, are stretched to their limit; and the coastal railway between Calvi and Ile Rousse is as busy as a big-city bus service. The lazier tourists prefer to lie on the beach, while the more energetic don their walking boots to explore the neighbouring mountains. There are opportunities for tennis and minigolf, horse-riding and go-cart riding, and a thriving night-life in the bars and clubs.

Calvi is worth a visit just to look at. The citadel is a beautiful

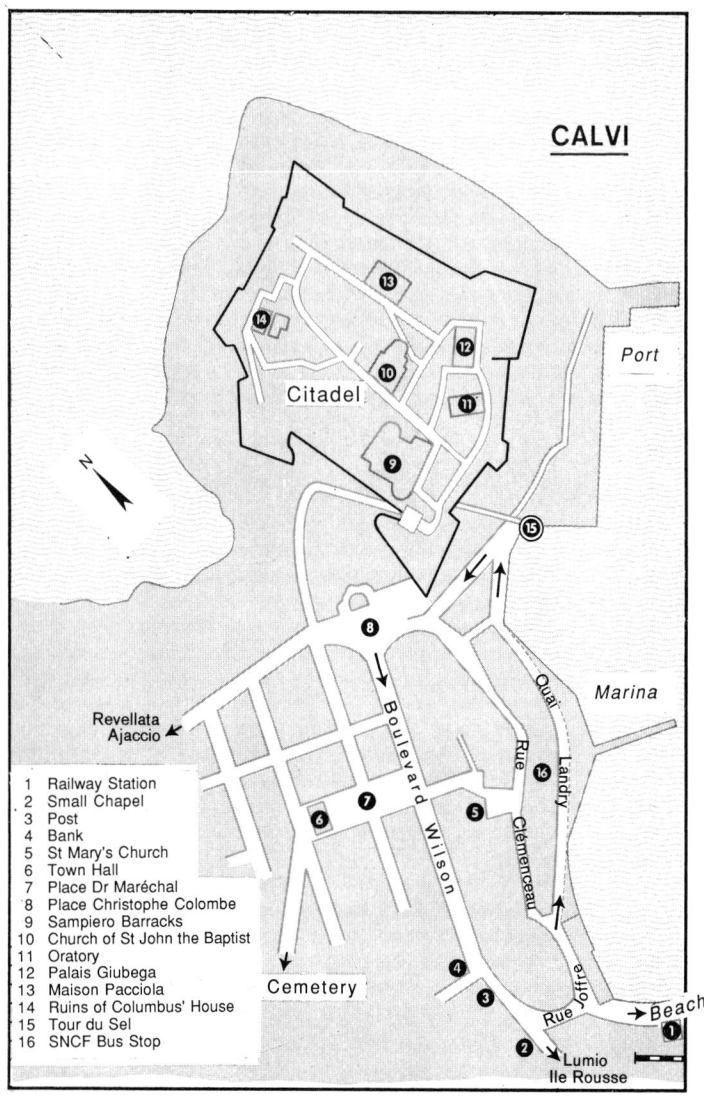

CALVI

Port

Citadel

Marina

Revellata
Ajaccio

1 Railway Station
2 Small Chapel
3 Post
4 Bank
5 St Mary's Church
6 Town Hall
7 Place Dr Maréchal
8 Place Christophe Colombe
9 Sampiero Barracks
10 Church of St John the Baptist
11 Oratory
12 Palais Giubega
13 Maison Pacciola
14 Ruins of Columbus' House
15 Tour du Sel
16 SNCF Bus Stop

Boulevard Wilson

Quai Landry

Rue Clémenceau

Rue Joffre

Cemetery

Beach

Lumio
Ile Rousse

sight from a distance, and the streets have a wonderful atmosphere that combines the old with the new. The suggested route
begins at the railway station, which lies at the end of the beach,

The Genoese Citadel, Calvi

where the coast road comes in from Ile Rousse (see route 2).

Just across the main road is a lovely old fourteenth-century ⌘ chapel, which is raised about three metres above the newly-built road. The vaulting of an even older building is now visible by the roadside where it was previously buried underground. Nothing more is known for certain about this at present, but investigations are due to begin, which may indicate it to have been one of the very early Christian churches.

The route turns right into town along the Avenue de la République, which quickly becomes the Boulevard Wilson. On the first corner on the left are the post office and the bank, where currency can be exchanged. Then on the left a square opens out called the Place Dr Maréchal, at the far end of which is the **Town Hall**. This contains a number of beautiful paintings, including ⌘ three Rubens presented by Cardinal Fesch.

The Boulevard Wilson ends at the foot of the citadel, where it enters a broad square called the Place Christophe Colombe. There is a war memorial ahead, and a road comes in from the harbour to the right; the road to the left is the D81 west-coast road to Ajaccio (see route 1).

⌘   The **citadel** is also known as the old town or, more appropriately, the Haute-Ville ('upper town'), since the new town or Basse-Ville ('lower town') also contains some old buildings. The ramparts date back to 1545. The entrance was once protected by a drawbridge and portcullis, and above it is the proud Genoese inscription *Civitas Calvi semper fidelis*, meaning 'city of Calvi ever faithful'. Many of the old buildings have fallen into ruin; but there is a magnificent view from the top. To the east is the bay with the hills of Balagne and the mountains beyond; to the west is the rocky peninsula of Revellata.

⌘   Immediately to the left of the gate is the former **Governor's Palace**. Built in the eighteenth century, it is now known as the Sampiero Barracks and houses the Foreign Legion's parachute regiment.

     Behind the barracks and to the right of the Place des Armes is
⌘   the sixteenth-century cathedral of **St John the Baptist**, which stands on the highest point of the citadel. The ground plan of the original thirteenth-century structure was in the form of a Greek cross. This was burnt down in 1481, but its foundations were used for the present rather austere domed structure. This was built in 1528, badly damaged in 1553 and subsequently restored. Originally built as a parish church, it became the cathedral for the diocese of Sagone in 1576.

     The main altar is particularly beautiful; it goes back to the seventeenth century, and is made of multicoloured marble. Also of interest are the sixteenth-century white marble font and the triptych in the apse, which was created in about 1600 by Barbagelata of Genoa. The side chapels contain yet more treasures. In the chapel to the left of the choir is a sixteenth-century carved wooden Madonna from Seville. In the chapel to the right is an ebony crucifix known as the Christ of Miracles. During the siege of Calvi by Sampiero Corso with his French and Turkish reinforcements, the crucifix was carried around the ramparts of the citadel, and is supposed to have repelled the besieging armies. Also of interest are the box pews beneath the dome, which were reserved for the noble ladies of the town.

⌘   Further south towards the southern battlement is **St Anthony's Oratory**. Though restored, it is the only example of a Renaissance church in the whole of Corsica. Above the entrance is a stone relief carved in Genoese slate. The most interesting feature inside is a seventeenth-century wooden carving of God the Creator.

Modern Calvi

To the east of the oratory is the old bishop's palace. Originally built in the fifteenth century, it has been heavily restored and is now known as the **Palais Giubega**. The next building to the north along the eastern battlement is the **Maison Pacciola**, which is interesting for its marble steps and window decorations. Both buildings belonged to Napoléon's godfather Laurent Giubega, who in 1793 sheltered the Bonaparte family for a month when they fled here from Ajaccio, pursued by Paoli's troops for being loyal to France.

Further round on the north side of the citadel are the remains of another house where, according to a plaque, Christopher Columbus was born in 1441. There is much evidence, but no proof, that Columbus was born in Calvi. Visitors who arrive in the early evening are recommended to linger by the battlements nearby to watch the sun set over the Revellata Peninsula. The view makes a lovely photograph, with a clump of agaves in the foreground.

The steep cliffs bordering the Gulf of Revellata are beloved of divers and snorklers, who much prefer them to the shallow sandy beach along the Gulf of Calvi. In the middle of these cliffs is a small sandy cove called the Anse de Revellata, which can be reached via a path from the main road.

The route returns to the war memorial by the Place Christophe Colombe (where one is surprised not to find a statue of Columbus himself). To the left is a flight of steps going down to the Rue Clémenceau, which forms the main street of the old Basse-Ville. It is narrow and lined with tall, ugly buildings containing shops, bars, restaurants and hotels. Flights of steps or small alleyways lead off to the Boulevard Wilson above or to the harbour below.

By a square to the right about half-way along the Rue Clémenceau is the church of **St Mary of the Assumption**, which was built in the eighteenth century. It is hexagonal in plan, and the dome is topped by a typical Baroque lantern. The tall bell tower is more Gothic in form, with its narrow steeple surrounded by four small corner spires.

The Rue Clémenceau turns into the Rue Joffre, and re-enters the Avenue de la République just before the railway station (see above). The Rue Clémenceau effectively forms one branch of the Rue Joffre, the other branch being the Quai Landry, which goes down to the harbour. Most of the local tourist offices are along the Quai Landry and the Rue Joffre.

The Quai Landry is lined with cafés and souvenir shops. On the left is the main terminus for the SNCF buses, while on the right is the marina or *quai de plaisance*, where the yachts and the pleasure boats dock. Brightly-painted fishing boats add to the colourful scene, and there is a general air of bustle and holiday spirit.

Below the citadel at the end of the quay is the **Tour du Cel** — a massive round tower that was once used for storing salt. Built in the fifteenth century, it is linked to the citadel by a wall that runs up under the battlements. A gateway in this wall leads through to the quay where the boats from the French mainland dock. The road, meanwhile, bends sharply to the left and climbs steeply to the Place Christophe Colombe.

Excursions from Calvi

Calvi Beach
The beach stretches along the bay to the east of the town, and is a good place for a walk, being anything between 6km and 12km in length. It is lined to the south by long rows of hotels.

The Church of Madonna della Serra

Madonna della Serra (6km)

The pilgrimage church of Madonna della Serra is situated on a
rocky summit above the town at a height of 216m. It can be
reached via the D81 coast road to Ajaccio. About 4km from Calvi
there is a left turn along a twisty road leading up to the summit
(2km). It can also be reached on foot, being about forty minutes'
walk from Calvi along a path that approaches from the opposite
direction via the cemetery and Fort Charlet.

Though originally built in the fifteenth century, the church has
been destroyed and rebuilt several times. The present building
goes back to the nineteenth century. The church is the subject of
an annual event on the Sunday next after 8 September, known as
the Festival of the Madonna, in which a ceremonial procession
comes up the hill from Calvi. The view from the top is very
attractive, and there are some interesting *tafoni* to be seen.

Revellata Peninsula (about 8km)

The path to the Revellata Peninsula comes off the Ajaccio road
about 1½km west of Calvi. It runs the whole length of the coast as
far as the lighthouse (102m) on the red cliffs at the end of the
peninsula (about two hours' walk). Those with less time may
prefer to drive further along the road as far as the turning for

Madonna della Serra (4km), and take a small road to the right. The
lighthouse is then about 3km on foot from the end of the road.

The lighthouse provides a quite unusual view of Calvi, in which
the mountains form the background instead of the sea. The
irregular cliffs along the west side of the peninsula hide a number
of beautiful grottos, of which the best-known is that of the **Veaux
Marins**. There are boat trips to here from Calvi marina, provided
the sea is sufficiently calm.

Bonifato Mountains (22km)
The route leaves Calvi along the N197 coast road to Ile Rousse,
and turns off past the international airport. It continues along the
broad valley of the Figarella, with views of Montemaggiore and
Calenzana on the hills of Balagne to the left. The valley slopes
were once covered with *maquis*, but have now been turned over to
vineyards.

The mountains become higher and higher. The road is hardly
any steeper, but becomes noticeably twistier as it runs along the
hillside above the course of the river. Pine forests appear above
the deciduous woodlands, and behind them the peaks rise almost
sheer to heights of up to 2,000m. The rocky outcrops near the
road reveal interesting *tafoni* formations.

Eventually the road passes a forest house on the slopes to the
right, and then immediately crosses a bridge over a stream that
goes down into the Figarella. About 100m further on, the road
ends by a restaurant (536m). A small path leads down to the
Figarella itself, which at the height of summer has about enough
water for paddling, though in early June it makes an ideal bathing
spot. The clear mountain water flows over stones of various sizes
that pile up into interesting formations.

Calenzana and Montemaggiore (45km)
This excursion forms a kind of mini **Balagne** tour. The first
section to Calenzana (13km) begins on the N197 coast road to Ile
Rousse. About 4¹/₂km from Calvi, there is a right turn along the
D151, which runs up the valley of the Bartasca to Calenzana.

Calenzana (300m) is situated on a slope overlooking the
valley. With a population of 300, it is the largest village in western
Balagne, where the local honey is said to be particularly good.
Calenzana is at the north-western end of a famous mountain path
known as the Grande Randonnée or GR20, which goes all the way
through the mountains to Conca near Ste Lucie de Porto-Vecchio

Calvi

The harbour at Calvi

Seashore near St Florent

Sant' Antonino

Bonifato mountains

---

in south-eastern Corsica.

The church of St Blaise, known as La Collegiata, was built in ⌘
about 1700 on the site of an older building. The interior is full of

beautiful multicoloured marble, and the free-standing bell tower includes some lovely Baroque decorations. Below the churchyard is the Campo Santo dei Tedeschi or German Cemetery. The soldiers buried here were among the reinforcements sent by the Austrian emperor to support the Genoese during the second Corsican rebellion of 1732.

The road continues towards Zilia. Just outside Calenzana there is a path off to the right, which first follows the course of the Secco and eventually goes up to the summit of **Monte Grosso** (1,941m). The reward of 4 hours' climb is a magnificent view of the Monte Cinto massif and the Forêt de Tartagine in the valley beneath.

To the left of the road, about 1km from Calenzana, is the famous pilgrimage church of Sta Restituta. Though originally Romanesque, it reveals an interesting mixture of architectural styles. The main part of the building dates back to the fifteenth century, when the original structure was heavily restored. Mounted on the side walls are some interesting china bowls, which were popular in Tuscany at the time. The side chapels in the choir are late Romanesque or Gothic.

In 1951 a sarcophagus was found in the crypt, containing the mortal remains of Sta Restituta and the five other martyrs who were executed with her in Calvi in AD 225. The sarcophagus is made of Carrara marble, and was probably made in the fourth century. The church above has a memorial to Sta Restituta, but this only dates back to the Middle Ages.

An adjoining building contains a 2.4m high menhir that was found by a shepherd in the countryside nearby. A head is clearly recognisable at the top, and there is a legend that says it was a guardsman who was turned to stone during the barbarian invasions at the end of the Roman empire.

The road skirts the valley slopes as it continues via Zilia to **Montemaggiore** (11km), which can be seen from Calvi at night. Montemaggiore (400m) clings to the terraces on the hillside, high up above the valley. There are some beautiful views down to the coast and across the valley to Calenzana.

There is a direct route from here back to Calvi. Alternatively, one can continue along the road over the Col de Salvi to Cateri (7km). Not far along this road from Montemaggiore is a turning signposted to the tiny Romanesque chapel of St Rainier, which was built in the thirteenth century out of a mixture of dark and light stone.

At **Cateri** the route comes to a crossroads. The road straight on goes via Corbara (11km) to Ile Rousse; a right turn along the D71 takes one in the direction of Belgodère (both these routes are described in the section on Balagne below). The present route goes left along the D71 to Lumio (7½km), and returns along the coast road to Calvi (another 10km).

A Further Excursion

The Balagne Region

Balagne forms the hinterland to Corsica's north-western coast. Bordered to the south by the high mountains of central Corsica, this fertile and hilly region is ideal for excursions from coastal resorts between Calvi and Ile Rousse. Its numerous small villages are linked by narrow, twisting roads. The scenery is varied, including orchards and olive groves, pasture and *maquis*, and offers an interesting alternative to sunbathing or aquatic sports.

Most of the villages are served by buses, and there are extra local services in the summer along the railway line between Calvi and Ponte Leccia, providing numerous starting points for walkers and climbers. Car and moped riders have a choice of several possible round trips.

Visitors staying on the coast between Calvi and Algajola are recommended to start from Lumio, 10km east of Calvi, where the D71 leaves the coast road towards Belgodère (32km).

The village of **Lumio** (220m; population 300) is on the hillside overlooking the road, but the marvellous view makes it well worth the short detour. To the west is the flat coastal plain that adjoins the Gulf of Calvi, with the mountains behind. The ruined tower on the nearby **Capo d'Occi** (563m) is the best viewing point in the area. The village itself has an interesting church with a modern façade; the old Baroque bell tower is separate, and is clearly visible from the road. To the south is the cemetery chapel, which though originally Romanesque has been heavily restored in other styles.

The D71 goes through Lavatoggio and past the old abbey of Marcasso to **Cateri** (8km), where the most interesting building is the small Romanesque chapel of San Cesaréo.

At Cateri the D71 crosses the road from Ile Rousse and Corbara to Calenzana (18km; see excursion above). Visitors

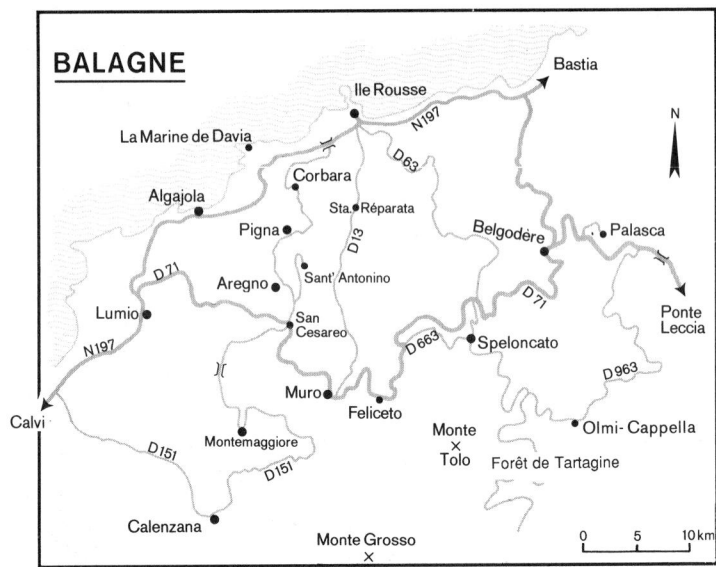

BALAGNE

staying on the coast between Algajola and Ile Rousse are recommended to leave the coast road near Corbara and come across to Cateri along this alternative route, passing some very interesting places on the way.

The village of **Corbara** (179m; population 500) is within walking distance of Ile Rousse, and clings to the hillside above the road. It has a lovely Baroque church, and is overlooked by the former residence of the local lord Guido Savelli, which though built in the ninth century is still partially complete. The large cemetery to the south is a reminder of the fact that Corbara was once a town. Corbara's most famous inhabitant was a woman who was kidnapped by Moroccan pirates, but who, because of her great beauty, eventually became Empress Davia of Morocco — hence the name of the nearby coastal village of **Marine de Davia**.

Corbara Abbey is 2km south of Corbara overlooking the road, and is 7km walk from Ile Rousse. It was originally built as an orphanage, but 25 years later (in 1456) it was turned into a Franciscan monastery. Like all other monasteries on the island, it was destroyed during the French Revolution. But in 1857 it came into the hands of the Dominicans, who restored and extended it. Nowadays there are chamber concerts here during the island's

Sleepy street, Corbara

August music festival. A small cave in the garden has been turned into a chapel, with an altar made of a beautiful white stone from the mountains of Ste Baume in Provence.

To the north of the abbey is **Monte Sant' Angelo** (564m), which takes about three quarters of an hour to climb. In clear weather the whole of the north coast is visible as far as Cap

Baroque church, Corbara

Corse. Walkers from Ile Rousse may return via a different route through Palmento or Santa Reparata-di-Balagna. There is also a short cut for walkers to Sant' Antonino (see below), though the road route is in many ways more beautiful.

1km to the south of Corbara Abbey, and just off the road to Cateri, is the village of **Pigna**. Its church is unusual in having domes on both the towers above the façade. This is probably a sign of the Moorish influence that is visible throughout Balagne. Visitors are recommended to go through a gate in the wall to the left of the church under a sign saying *Casa Paesana/Maison Artisanat* '. This leads to a lovely collection of handicrafts — something that is all too rare on Corsica.

2km further along the road is the lovely little cemetery church of **Aregno**. It was built in the fourteenth century out of an interesting combination of pale limestone and blue slate, and is thus similar to St Michel near Murato. Even without the bell tower, the façade is if anything more beautiful, with its integral columns and arches. There are statues of various exotic animals, with two men either side of the door arch, one clothed and one naked. Also of interest are two lovely fifteenth-century frescos.

Barely 1km further on, and about 1km from the crossroads at **Cateri**, there is a turning along a small side road (2km) to what is probably the most remarkable site in the whole of Balagne. **Sant'** ⌘ **Antonino** (497m) is visible from some distance away, being perched on the summit of a steep hill. Its present population is about 150. No reason has been found as to why it should have been named after a little-known tribune in the Syrian legion who was martyred in the fourth century.

Sant' Antonino was founded by a member of the Savelli family from Rome, who in the ninth century built a castle on this most Corsican of Corsican sites on the top of a rock. Both Savelli and a member of another influential Roman family that had rebelled against the Pope were called upon by Charlemagne to guard Corsica against attack from the Saracens. So Savelli settled in the north while the other one settled in the south.

In the course of time a small settlement grew up around the castle, clinging for protection to the rocks immediately below it. No wonder that the place was later nicknamed 'the eyrie'! Sant' Antonino was destroyed several times. For hardly had the Saracens gone than the Pisans and the Genoese began to vie for supremacy.

The Genoese wanted the whole island for themselves, but faced fierce opposition from some of the Corsican nobility, to whom these two Roman families now belonged. The local populace kept changing sides, depending on the way things were going. In 1485 the people of Sant' Antonino set their lord's house alight and forced him to flee for his life. Being on the side of the Genoese, he fled to Bastia and asked them for assistance. The Genoese sent troops to Sant' Antonino, who to their surprise were warmly received and given quarters to stay in. But none of them escaped alive. Two years later the Genoese embarked on a ferocious campaign of revenge.

1553 saw another event that affected Sant' Antonino. The Genoese at Calvi were under siege from Sampiero Corso with his French and Turkish reinforcements. Anton-Paolo Savelli hastened with an army from Sant' Antonino to assist the Genoese. On the way there his own son was captured by the enemy forces, who told him, 'Give us the city and we'll give you back your son!' But he stood by the Genoese, and his son was killed as a result.

The present lordly residence still belongs to the Savelli family. Above the entrance is a stone from the original castle with the following inscription: 'Good luck to the man who greets you here! 1 June 813.' Anton-Paolo might well have doubted this on his return from a victorious Calvi in 1553.

The church is rather modern, and stands by an open square below the entrance to the village. The small road turns right here and goes round in a loop to enter the village from behind. Sant' Antonino is a maze of narrow streets that are often no more than flights of steps. The houses seem to be piled on top of each other, and many are derelict. But occasionally a donkey will poke its head round a corner or a cat will jump down from a wall. An old car wheel has been made into a flowerpot full of geraniums, creating a spot of colour in an otherwise drab scene. Some of the 'streets' turn out to be house entrances, forcing one to turn back. Behind some of the old shutters a television can be seen, or maybe a modern pram in the hallway.

In front of a restaurant in one of these dark streets is a modern wash basin with two taps, one with a red knob and the other with a blue one. But there is no running water; this needs to be pumped out of a tank nearby. Going through the restaurant, one is dazzled by the bright sunshine that floods in from the verandah. There is a magnificent view south across the hills and villages of Balagne to the snow-capped peaks beyond.

Immediately below the 'eyrie' is a little old chapel surrounded by cypress trees. From the top one can see northwards to the rounded summit of Monte Sant' Angelo, which is on about the same level as Sant' Antonino. To the left of it is the lower land bordering the coast, with resorts such as Marine de Davia, Algajola and Marine de Sant' Ambroggio.

There is another way up from the church by the square. Instead of taking the road, one can go left past an old chapel and along a narrow path that appears to enter the ground floor of one of the houses. It is in fact a kind of tunnel that zigzags up through the side of the hill before coming back out into the blinding light of day. This appears to have been part of the old castle vaults. Either side of a small doorway are some patterns in the stonework that are typical of the Carolingian period.

Visitors are reluctant to leave, and keep looking back from the

Ile Rousse from the beach

road at this lovely old village where time has stood still.

The route continues from Cateri along the D71 towards Belgodère (25km). It passes the narrow bell tower of Avapessa on the left, and after 4km arrives at **Muro** (300m; population 500) — a lovely little village in a lovely situation. The verandahs along the fronts of the houses show that the people are not poor, living in an area that is fertile and prosperous. There is a left turn along a small road that goes direct to Ile Rousse (14km).

Feliceto (300m) is 4km further along the D71. To the north of the village is a small chapel. A path leads off to the south to a rocky summit (903m) with a marvellous view.

After another 9km the road crosses the D63. A left turn takes one along a rather less interesting route to Ile Rousse. A right turn brings one up to Speloncato (3km), from which the D63 continues southwards towards the beautiful Forêt de Tartagine (see below).

Speloncato (600m) is perched on the summit of a hill, and is almost as old as Sant' Antonino. It is, however, somewhat larger, with a population of 250. The palace used to belong to a member of the Savelli family who was secretary to Pope Pius IV; it has now been turned into a hotel. The church is another fine example of the rich and beautiful Baroque churches that grace many of the villages in Corsica. Not far away is a small mineral spring with the remains of some Roman baths.

There is another good view from the top. The more energetic visitors may care to negotiate the summit of Monte Tolo (1,392m), which is 2 hours' climb away to the south. The view from here is even better, encompassing the whole of the north coast of Corsica. Those who would rather drive should take the D63 Forêt de Tartagine road to its highest point (1,105m), which provides some exciting scenery. If one continues along this road, one eventually arrives at Olmi-Cappella (13 1/2 km), which is described below.

Continuing from the crossroads along the D71, one arrives after 7km at **Belgodère** (310m; population 500), which is situated among the chestnut woods on the valley slope. The river at the bottom eventually comes out into a wide basin. Up above the village, a ruined castle stands guard among the cypress trees. It was built in about AD 1000 by Margrave Malaspina, who had been appointed governor by the Pope. There is a marvellous view from the top. Further down the hill is the nineteenth-century Château de la Costa, which is now used as a school. Its chapel is built out of the famous marble from Carrara. There is a ruined monastery nearby.

At Belgodère the road enters the main N197 Calvi-Ponte Leccia road. To the left it is only 7km to the coast at Lozari, and another 8km westwards to Ile Rousse (see route 2). To the right it is 33km to Ponte Leccia on the Corte-Bastia road (see route 5).

A short distance towards Ponte Leccia, there is a turning off the N197 for the old village of **Palasca**, which is famous for its beautiful pottery. 6 1/2 km from Belgodère, and just below the top of the Col de San Colombano, there is a right turn along the main access road to the **Forêt de Tartagine.** This beautiful wooded valley is particularly popular with visitors to Ile Rousse who want a change from the beach.

The road to the Forêt de Tartagine crosses three passes in the first 15km to Olmi-Cappella: the Bocca di u Prunu (746m), the Bocca Capanna (844m) and the Bocca a Croce (928m). Soon Monte Padro (2,393m) comes into view, forming the northern bulwark of the central Corsican massif. In front of it the Forêt de Tartagine stretches out along the slopes of the valley. It is probably the most beautiful valley on the whole island, full of oak and pine forests circled by mighty peaks.

At **Olmi-Cappella** (800m) the D63 comes in from Speloncato (see above). The road winds on for another 17km to the forest house (717m), where the forest proper begins. Situated by a bridge on the upper reaches of the River Tartagine, it is an ideal spot for camping. Trout fishing is only allowed below the bridge; but when the season is right, there are thousands of wild strawberries to be picked. The forest is full of paths through magnificent scenery.

The best walking route is the one to the top end of the valley, which goes over the bridge and turns right along the bank of the river. It takes about one and a half hours to cover the 5km to the end of the valley, where a fast stream comes down from the Col d'Ondella. The path crosses it and follows it up over the pass on the opposite bank.

To the right above the source of the Tartagine, the **Col de Tartagine** (1,852m) is just visible among the trees, flanked on either side by the double-peaked Capu a u Dente (2,032m) and Monte Corona (2,144m). The pass can be reached by turning right off the main path; it takes 3 hours to climb, plus another hour to the summit of Monte Corona. From the top one can look back along the valley, with Monte Padro to the right and Cap Corse in the far distance beyond. Looking in the opposite direction, there are the peaks of the Paglia Orba and Monte Cinto ranges to the left, and the coast around Calvi to the right.

9 CORTE

The Heart of Corsica

Corte (396m) is situated on a rocky outcrop above the valley of the Tavignano, next to its confluence with the Restonica. It is clustered around an old fortress on the top of the rock. One side of this rock falls sheer, while the other side slopes more gently, forming the site of the old town of Corte.

The town today has a population of 6,000. It is the centre of an agricultural area producing wine, tobacco, vegetables and olives. There is a small amount of industry based on the nearby marble quarries, the local marble being bluish with reddish veins.

Corte should really be the capital of Corsica, since its position in the central mountains gives it a much more Corsican feel than either of the two main coastal towns. It was the capital only from 1755–69, during the short period of independence under Pasquale Paoli. But Corte played a vital role in Corsica's many freedom struggles, and is rightly thought of as the island's spiritual centre.

The main street in the new town is the Cours Paoli, on the west side of which is the town hall. Somewhat to the left of this is a flight of steps leading down to the chapel of **Ste Croix**, which has a Baroque façade. At the northern end of the Cours Paoli is the Place du Duc de Padoue, which forms the centre of the new town. At the southern end is the Place Paoli, with a bronze statue of Paoli himself.

The Rue Scoliscia leads from the Place Paoli to the Place Gaffori — the main square of the old town. To the right of the square is a statue of General Gaffori, with his house behind it. Like other buildings in the town, it is pitted with bullet holes from the time of the Corsican freedom struggles. Further to the right the Rue de la Fontaine leads off to a small square with a fountain in the centre called the **Fontaine des Quatre Canons**. It is in the form of an obelisk, and is still the only water source for many of the houses around.

To the left of the Place Gaffori is the seventeenth-century

Corte

Church of the Annunciation, with its tall Baroque bell tower. ⌘
Inside are two lovely wooden tabernacles and a beautiful pulpit,
and the vestry contains a small white marble statue of the Virgin
Mary.

Behind the church is the chapel of St Theophilus of Corte,
while to the right of it a flight of steps leads up to the **Palais** ⌘
National. This was the seat of government under Pasquale
Paoli, whose study and bedroom are on show to the public. The
building also contains an interesting museum describing the
history and prehistory of Corsica.

Not far from here is the house where the Bonaparte family lived
before they moved to Ajaccio, and where their son Joseph was
born who later became king of Spain.

The steps to the left of the Palais National lead on up to the ⌘
castle, which, being a military headquarters, is closed to the
public. There is supposed to have been a small fort here as early
as the eleventh century. In 1420 it was turned into a large
stronghold by Vincentello d'Istria, count of Cinarca, who had been

Church of the Annunciation, Corte

made viceroy of Corsica by Alfonse V of Aragon.

Leading south from the Place Poilu by the Palais National is the Rue Balthasar Arrighi. If one carries on through a maze of narrow streets, it eventually leads to a round tower directly beneath the castle. This is known as Belvédère on account of the wonderful view from the top. A narrow path leads down from here to the river, which is spanned by an old Genoese bridge.

Excursions from Corte

Romanesque Churches and Roman Remains

2km to the north of Corte, just off the N193 Bastia road, is the church of Sta Mariona, whose twin apses are typical of Romanesque churches on Corsica.

2¹/₂km to the south-east, along a road off the N200 to Aléria, is the ruined church of San Giovanni or St Jean. This early Romanesque building has a small baptistry attached with a ground plan in the form of a Maltese cross.

Both of these sites include some old Roman remains, where valuable items are still being unearthed such as pottery, coins and bronze goods. This would tend to reinforce the theory put forward by an old historian that Corte was a Roman colony and the site of the battle that sparked off the third Punic war.

17½km from Corte along the N200 Aléria road, next to an old Genoese bridge, is another little church that goes back to 1002.

The Tavignano Gorge
This is 2 hours' walk from Corte along a path that begins by the chapel of Ste Croix (see above). The path runs along the north bank of the river through some rough and rocky terrain.

The Restonica Valley (17km)
This gorgeous valley runs up into the mountains to the south-west of Corte. It is reached via the D623 — a narrow, twisty road leading from the southern exit of the town. It runs past a marble quarry and through several narrow, rocky defiles called the **Gorges de la Restonica.** It ends at the top of the valley (1,300m) at the foot of Punta alle Porte (2,313m) and Monte Rotondo (2,622m).

Two lakes on the slopes of Punta alle Porte are favourite destinations for hill-walkers. The **Lac de Melo** (1,711m) is an easy hour's climb up a stony path that becomes steep at the top. The **Lac de Capitello** (1,927m) must be the most beautiful lake in Corsica. It is 200m or so higher, requiring another hour's climb, and can be reached from the Lac de Melo via a path (shown by stone markers) that goes up to the right beside a stream.

Further Excursions

The Niolo Region

At one time Niolo was very much off the beaten track, and was the exclusive domain of shepherds and crofters. But since the D84 was built over the Col de Vergio, it has come within striking distance of west-coast resorts such as Porto. The majority of organised trips are to Calacuccia, 27km from Corte, which can

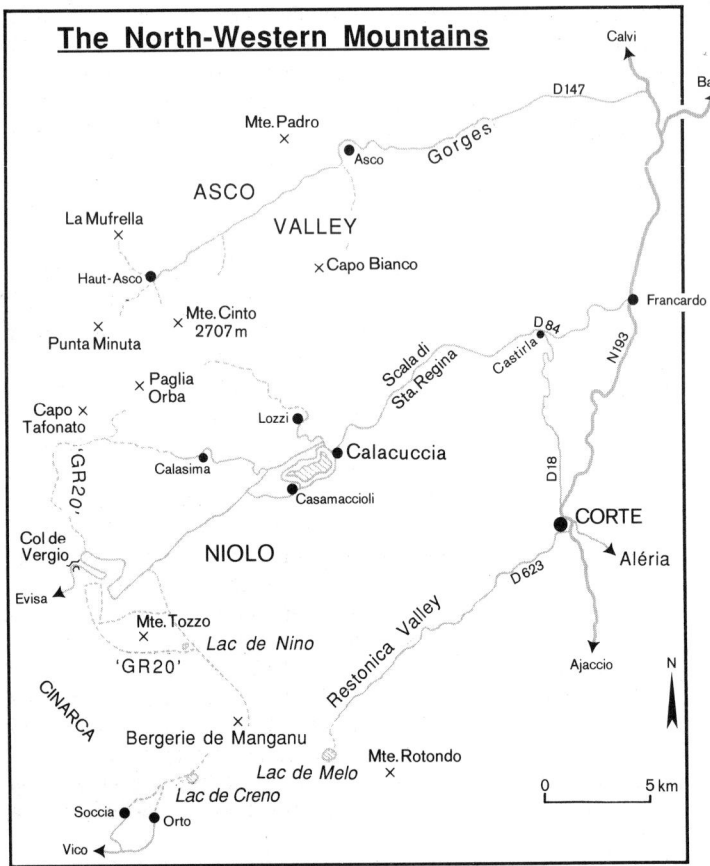

The North-Western Mountains

Calvi

D147

Bastia

Mte. Padro
×

Asco   Gorges

ASCO

VALLEY

La Mufrella
×

×Capo Bianco

Haut-Asco ●

D84

Francardo ●

Mte. Cinto
× 2707 m

Scala di Sta. Regina

Castirla

N193

×
Punta Minuta

×Paglia
Orba

Capo ×
Tafonato

Lozzi ●

●Calacuccia

GR20

Calasima ●

D18

Casamaccioli ●

Col de
Vergio

NIOLO

●CORTE

Restonica Valley

Aléria

Evisa ◀

Mte. Tozzo
×   Lac de Nino

D623

'GR20'

CINARCA

Ajaccio

N

Mte. Rotondo

Bergerie de Manganu ×

Lac de Melo   ×

Soccia ●

Lac de Creno
● Orto

0   5 km

Vico ◀

also be used as a base for exploring the mountains around.

The route goes due north from Corte along the D18. It climbs for 5km up the Col d'Ominanda (657m), then drops down for the next 7km until it comes to a bridge over the Golo at **Pont de Castirla.** At this point it joins the D84, which comes up from Francardo on the N193, 6km to the east (see route 5), and carries on through Niolo and over the Col de Vergio to Cinarca (see page 85ff).

5km from the bridge, the road comes to the famous **Scala di Sta Regina,** where the River Golo forces its way through a gorge 500m deep and 8km long. Its flow is further interrupted by enormous boulders. Depending on the weather and the time of day, the rocks create a wonderful variety of colours, from reddish yellow to lilac. Nature is manifested in all its beauty and strength.

The road passes a large hydroelectric power station that is visible from the bridge far behind. At the top end of the gorge is a dam with a large reservoir behind it, further enhancing the landscape. The valley becomes broader again, and its lower slopes are so gentle as to create the effect of a plateau. The grassy slopes are used mainly for pasture.

2km from the dam is the popular mountain resort of **Cala-cuccia** (830m). With 1,200 resident inhabitants, it is Niolo's main centre of population. There is not much to see in Calacuccia itself, apart from a carved wooden statue of Christ in St Peter's Church — a marvellous example of the Corsican wood-carving tradition that is still very much practised in Niolo.

From Calacuccia a small road leads off to the right to **Calasima** (7km), which at 1,095m is the highest village on the island. From Calacuccia one can see Corsica's highest peak, Monte Cinto, whereas from Calasima it is her most beautiful mountain, **Paglia Orba** (2,525m), that is visible. In order to get an even better view, one can continue on foot along an old forest path by a stream to the Grotte des Anges (4km).

Monte Cinto (2,707m) when viewed from the south is not nearly as impressive as Paglia Orba. Neither is Corsica's highest peak very difficult to climb from this side. The plateau below the summit (1,500m) is easily accessible to ramblers, being about three hours' walk from Calacuccia. If one drives up through Lozzi and then as far as the road goes, it is only 40 minutes' walk to the mountain hut at Bicarello, plus another hour to the foot of the peak.

About 1½km west of Calacuccia along the D84, there is a dolmen in a field to the left of the road. The stones have eroded to create a shape like some fabulous beast. A little further along on the right is an old Franciscan monastery. There is a restaurant by the road, and a sign pointing up the road to an archaeological museum. The museum is at the next village, called **Albertacce** (870m), which also has a little old church and an old well built out of pebbles from the river in an interesting mosaic pattern. The chestnut trees around here are often mixed with walnut trees.

It is 20km further to the Col de Vergio. The road goes for 14km through one of the island's largest forests, the Forêt de Valdo-Niello. It includes an enormous variety of trees — beeches,

Lac de Nino

birches, and especially conifers such as larches and Corsican pines.

About 9km after Albertacce, the road comes to a forest house called Popaja. Visitors may park here and have a walk through the forest. More energetic walkers may like to carry on to the **Lac de Nino** (1,700m), which is 3 hours' walk up the mountainside. The source of the River Tavignano, it is situated in a glacial trough and surrounded by wild, rocky scenery.

The road winds up the mountainside to the **Col de Vergio** (12km), which at 1,464m is Corsica's highest road pass. 2km before the summit, the road comes to a large hotel, which is used as a skiing centre in the winter and as a ramblers' centre in the summer. The most popular route for hill-walkers is a 7–hour circular route from the hotel, which includes the Lac de Nino (see above). A famous mountain path also passes through here — the so-called Grande Randonnée or GR20, which crosses the island from Calenzana in the north-west to Conca in the south-east. Visitors are recommended to walk along it for at least a short distance. The mountains and forests make an unforgettable sight as one gazes back along the valley towards Calacuccia.

Across the reservoir from Calacuccia is **Casamaccioli** (868m), famous for the feast of the Nativity of the Virgin, which takes place from 8 to 10 September every year. Though a serious religious event, it is also a folk festival, with opportunities for fun and merrymaking. First a statue of the Virgin Mary is processed around the village in a traditional dance called the Granitola or 'snail' because of the spiralling movements involved. The procession is followed by an extemporary singing and poetry competition, with contestants from all over the island.

For the rest of the year, the statue is kept in the Church of the Nativity. Its alleged miraculous powers attract pilgrims from all over Corsica. The village itself is beautifully situated at the south-western end of the reservoir, with a magnificent view across the valley to the Monte Cinto range, which divides Niolo from the Asco Valley to the north.

The Asco Valley

The Asco Valley is about 30km long, and runs deep into the Monte Cinto massif. The top end of the valley is dominated by Monte Cinto itself, which at 2,707m is Corsica's highest peak. The valley floor and the slopes either side are partly covered in pinewoods and juniper shrublands, and are partly used for pasture. The valley is renowned for its honey and its cheese.

The road into the valley comes off the N197 Ponte Leccia-Calvi road 2km north of Ponte Leccia (see route 5). The village of Asco itself is about 16km up the valley from the junction. For the 9km leading up to Asco, the river forces its way through the impressive Asco Gorge. The road is often cut out of the bare rock, and the cliffs tower above the river to breathtaking heights of up to 900m. The rock is variously coloured, and in places has been eroded into fascinating *tafoni* formations.

Asco (620m) is one of the oldest villages in Corsica. It has a population of 400, and clings to the hillside above the River Asco. Apart from the small seventeenth-century church of St Michel, there is the much older chapel of Sant' Angelo, which is further away up the mountainside (3km).

The old Genoese bridge below the village marks the point where the river changes name. It is the Stranciacone from its source as far as the bridge, and becomes the Asco from here downstream. Across the bridge is a path leading up into the mountains. It goes up to the left of a stream called the Pinnera to a mountain hut called the Bergerie de Pinnera (941m).

The road continues westwards from Asco along the course of the Stranciacone, and runs for 15km through the beautiful Forêt de Carrozzica. It first crosses to the south bank of the river; then about half-way through the forest it goes over a stream called the Manica. A path goes off just before the bridge, which follows the stream up to the Bergerie de Manica. It is a difficult hour and a half's climb up an old forest path that often resembles a dried-up stream. But the glorious scenery makes it well worth the effort. The main ridge of Monte Cinto soon comes into view. The path continues right up to the summit, which from this side is accessible only to experienced mountaineers.

2km further along the road is a monument to the foreign legionaries who built the remaining 5km section of the road between 1963 and 1964. The road soon emerges from the forest onto the **Stagno Plateau** (1,422m), where the valley ends in one of the most beautiful landscapes in Corsica. It is surrounded by towering peaks up to 2,500m high — Capo Larghia, Capo Rosso and Punta Minuta.

The entrance to the car park is graced by a memorial to Felix von Cube — a doctor from Stuttgart in Germany, who in about 1900 was the first person to explore the Corsican mountain ranges. The famous mountain path called the Grande Randonnée or GR20 runs across the mountainside high above the valley. The nearby *Haut-Asco* hotel is one of the few winter sports centres to be found on a Mediterranean island. A 1,300m long ski-lift links it to the ski slopes 250m above. But although skiing is becoming increasingly popular here, the walking and climbing season is considerably longer.

Two walking routes are especially recommended. The first goes along a moraine to the left, following the path to the Col de Borba, which is marked out by stones and red posts. It passes the upper reaches of the Stranciacone, and runs up beside another stream to **Trimbolacciu** — a glacial basin high up the mountainside that shows nature at its most beautiful and unspoilt. Coming back down, one can see the Lac de Stagno across to the left, provided it has not dried up during the summer.

The second route is to the **Lac de Stagno** itself. The path first goes up under the ski-lift. Near the top of the lift (between the ninth and tenth masts), there is a path to the right going up to the lake, which is in a small basin below the summit of Capo Stranciacone. It often dries up during the summer, but the landscape is nonetheless beautiful. Alternatively one can carry on to the top of the ski-lift, and continue along the same path to the Col de Stranciacone (1,987m). This is 2 hours' climb from the bottom, and provides a magnificent view of the rocky peaks and the forested valleys between.

10 PORTO-VECCHIO

Holiday Centre in the South-East

The old town of Porto-Vecchio was built on a 70m high rock at the south-western end of the longish inlet now named after it. Like other Corsican towns, it began as a Genoese fortress, built in the sixteenth century to protect what was already a well-sheltered natural harbour. A few of the original structures still remain, including sections of the wall, five towers, the old harbour gate and the old banqueting hall.

On the approach to the town there are views along the coast and inland to the Forêt de l'Ospédale and the Aiguilles de Bavella. There is a nice walk along the old city walls to a lookout point in front of the old harbour gate or **Porte Génoise**. From here one can see over the harbour, with its bright medley of fishing, merchant and pleasure boats, to the saltpans on the Stabiacco delta beyond. These are the only saltworks on Corsica, and are open to the public.

The town today has a population of 5,600, most of whom work in the harbour or in the cork industry. Its only major tourist amenity is the marvellous marina. Most of the other tourist facilities are to be found near the beaches along the coast.

The most interesting building in the town is the Church of **Ste Croix** by the market place, which was built in the nineteenth century to replace a much older building. The ceiling is particularly interesting, having been painted to look like wooden panelling. The altar consists of an enormous table, with an impressive painting on the wall behind it.

Excursions from Porto-Vecchio

The Coastline to the North (40km)
The route goes round the Golfo di Sogno (or Baie de Stagnolo) and via Cala Rossa to the lighthouse on the Punte de St Cyprien, then continues around the bays of St Cyprien and Pinarello to Ste

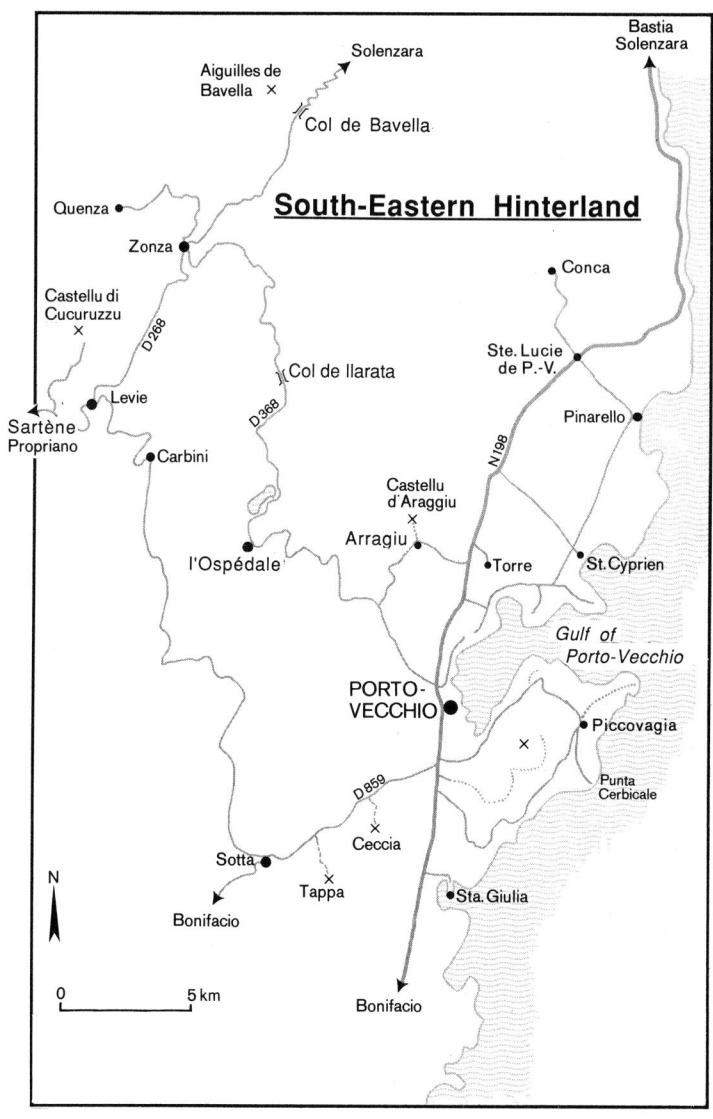

Aiguilles de Bavella ×

Solenzara

Col de Bavella

Bastia
Solenzara

South-Eastern Hinterland

Quenza ●

Zonza ●

Conca ●

Castellu di
Cucuruzzu
×

D268

Ste. Lucie
de P.-V.

Levie ●

Col de Ilarata

D368

Pinarello ●

Sartène
Propriano

Carbini ●

Castellu
d'Araggiu
×

N198

l'Ospédale ●

Arragiu

Torre ●

St. Cyprien ●

Gulf of
Porto-Vecchio

PORTO-
VECCHIO ●

Piccovagia ●

×

Punta
Cerbicale

D859

×
Ceccia

Sotta ●

N

×
Tappa

Sta. Giulia ●

Bonifacio

0   5 km

Bonifacio

Beach at Porto-Vecchio

Lucie de Porto-Vecchio, and returns to the town via the main road.

The Coastline to the South (26km)
The route takes the main road due south across the **Chiappa Peninsula**, and turns left for the pretty village of Bocca dell' Oro, nestling between the hills and the sea. It turns north along the coast of the peninsula via the Plage de Palombaggia to the Punte Cerbicale, with its view of the uninhabited Iles Cerbicales. It then continues via Piccovagia to the lighthouse on the Punte de la Chiappa, and returns to Porto-Vecchio along the bay.

A range of hills runs the whole length of the peninsula (325m). A path runs along the crest, providing some wonderful views.

Forêt de l'Ospédale (15km)
See **Bavella** on page 157.

Bonifacio (27km)
This excursion goes along the last section of the east-coast route (see route 3). In the first 6km, there are turnings to the left to the Chiappa Peninsula and Sta Giulia. There is also a right turn along

the D859, which goes via Sotta and Figari to join the N196 Bonifacio-Sartène road (see route 4). This can be used as an alternative route back from Bonifacio to Porto-Vecchio. Bonifacio itself is described on page 175.

Excursions into the Past

Porto-Vecchio is in the middle of the area where the ancient Bronze Age Torrean civilisation first settled on Corsica in the middle of the second millenium BC. A large number of their sites have been discovered here, and are the subject of continuing archaeological investigations. The most interesting sites are Castellu d'Arraggiu and Cucuruzzu.

Castellu d'Araggiu

This site is very close to Porto-Vecchio. The two hamlets that make up the village of Araggiu can be reached via a right turn off the D368 Zonza road (9km) or a left turn off the N198 Bastia road (8km). The Castellu d'Araggiu site is 20 minutes' walk from either hamlet along a signposted path. Apart from the good view, the site provides some fascinating insights into the past.

Castellu d'Araggiu consists of a round fortification on a hill (250m), which served as a refuge for the nearby villagers at times of danger. According to archaeological evidence, it was originally just a temple, and was only later extended to include an observation post. Later still a dwelling was added where the 'high priest' or 'officer in charge' might have lived.

The site provided a good view of the harbour, where boats might be observed entering and leaving. But no defences were needed until the Torreans began to colonise the rest of the island, and came under attack from the Megalithic people that were being displaced.

The fortification is about 120m in circumference. The entrance is on the eastern side, and consists of a covered corridor built of enormous stone slabs. Immediately to the right of it is a guard chamber with a ceiling slab weighing as much as two tonnes. It consists of a circular chamber with smaller rooms leading off it.

The temple is in a somewhat raised position to the left, in the south-western corner of the site. It consists of a circular, tower-like structure. The entrance is to the south-west, with a lookout platform to the south-east. The inner chamber was originally protected by a vaulted stone ceiling.

Torre (7½km)

⌘ This tower temple is situated on a hill next to the small village of Torre, just off the N198 Bastia road (see route 3). It is unusual in not having a chamber inside, but a corridor with three branches going off it.

Ceccia (4½km)

The village of Ceccia is south-west of Porto-Vecchio, just off the D859 Sotta road (see above). The lovely little tower temple is 20
⌘ minutes' walk away along a path leading up from the village. Built in 1,323 BC, it is interesting in having no surrounding fortifications, though it was probably used as a lookout tower as well as a temple.

  The tower is built on top of a large rock. The temple chamber measures no more than 2m in diameter, and is entered via a staircase going down from the terraced roof. This in turn appears to have been reached using a ladder.

Tappa (6km)

⌘ The Torrean site of Tappa is only 1km from Ceccia, but is half an hour's walk from the D859 Sotta road along a broad path through a vineyard. The site itself is situated on an area of irregular rocky terrain, and is easiest to approach from the left.

  It is an example of a fortification that is not situated in a particularly commanding position. But the terrain has been used to advantage in that the rocks on the ground have been worked into the structure of the walls.

  The temple itself has an internal diameter of 4½m, and is built on the highest point of the site. The fortifications below enclose a total area of half a hectare. The dwellings were lower down still, creating a complex three-layered structure.

  Tappa was probably the oldest Torrean settlement. The site also includes traces of much earlier human habitation going back to the fourth millennium BC.

Levie (50km)

Levie is 9½km south-west of Zonza along the D268 Sartène road (see page 160). Its museum is of particular interest to archaeo-
⌘ logy buffs, and should be visited in conjunction with the ancient Torrean sites of Cucuruzzu and Capula (see below).

Cucuruzzu

Castellu di Cucuruzzu (57km)

This fascinating site is about 7km from Levie (see above), and is signposted off the D268 Sartène road. It is 15 minutes' walk from the car park along a narrow, rough path through dense woodland where cows often stray.

The Torrean fortification of Castellu di Cucuruzzu is very similar to Castellu d'Araggiu. The site is spread out across the top of a mountain ridge (900m), which looks out up a wooded valley to the Aiguilles de Bavella in the distance.

The foundations of dwellings have been discovered within an area of about a hectare surrounded by a small protective wall. They have yet to be fully investigated, but have been attributed to both a Torrean and a sub-Torrean period of settlement, which together lasted for a total of 500 years from 1,400 to 900 BC.

The fortress proper measures a total of 30m by 40m. The entrance is on the west side, and has been hewn out of an enormous rock, demonstrating yet again how the Torrean builders took advantage of naturally-occurring features. The fortification walls are between 2m and 5m thick; they include a protected walkway with loopholes, and integral chambers both at and below ground level. A reserve store of catapult stones has also been found here.

The tower temple is on the east side at the back, at the highest and steepest point on the site. It is entered from the east along a corridor with two niches off it. There is a vast slab over the entrance with a relieving triangle above it. The inner chamber still retains its original vaulted stone ceiling — the only surviving Corsican example of a feature that has been lost from all the other Torrean sites on the island. The floor reveals traces of burning, indicating the probable use of burnt offerings.

The foundations of a dwelling have been discovered in a circle of naturally-occurring rocks immediately below the temple. This probably belonged to the 'high priest' or 'officer in charge' of the site.

Capula (57km)

The Capula site is very close to Castellu di Cucuruzzu (see above). Visitors should follow a forest track from the Cucuruzzu car park for about 100m, then turn along a small signposted path which runs for another 150m through an area of thickets and boulders.

Recent investigations have shown Capula to be extremely interesting from an archaeological point of view. The many layers of remains reveal evidence of settlement here for as long as 6,000 or maybe even 9,000 years, during a period lasting from the Middle Stone Age down to the Middle Ages.

One particularly significant find was the discovery of two fragments of a menhir on which a sword is clearly distinguishable. Known as the Paladin, it was found immediately below the Torrean fortifications. It not only indicates the existence here of a pre-Torrean Megalithic settlement, but also reveals that the two peoples must have come into conflict.

At the back of the site, again at the highest and steepest point, are the remains of a Torrean tower temple. There is a view across to Castellu di Cucuruzzu, with some unusual rock formations nearby. The strange and fascinating landscape adds to the aura of mystery that surrounds these ancient remains.

Forest and mountains of Bavella

A Further Excursion

The Bavella Region

The name Bavella has almost become a byword for Corsica. Visitors flock here to see the amazing Aiguilles de Bavella, to experience the dramatic mountain scenery, and to breathe in the wonderful forest scents.

The Bavella Mountains are less than 2,000m high, but are nonetheless often compared to the Dolomites. The Corsicans call them after their most distinctive feature, the **Aiguilles de Bavella** themselves, which they have wryly named the Torri d'Asinao, implying a resemblance to asses' ears! The Aiguilles are a series of bare, rocky needles. This truly magical sight is yet further enhanced by the ever-changing patterns of light and shade as the sun moves round and the clouds waft around among the peaks.

The **Col de Bavella** divides the mountain range into two

parts, of which the Aiguilles de Bavella form the main bastion to the north. The vegetation at the top of the pass consists mostly of grasses and mosses, as one might expect at 1,243m. But in places the harsh climate is softened by hardy pinewoods, making it an attractive location for campers.

The pass is 30km from **Solenzara** on the coast (see route 3). The D268 leaves Solenzara along the south bank of the river of the same name. After 12km it crosses the river, which at this stage opens out into several pebbly beaches that are easily accessible to bathers.

The road now climbs steeply in hairpins, passing a deep gorge to the right. There is warning sign showing a car falling off a precipice, which one assumes is intended to make drivers take care! After another 5km the road reaches the top of the **Col de Larone** (621m). The Col de Bavella is clearly visible ahead, flanked by peaks either side; but the road in between is hidden by thick forests. This is probably fortunate, since the motorist might well be tempted to turn back if he could actually see it! It first drops down, and then climbs through what seems like an interminable succession of twists and hairpins — though the 10km seem less to those coming in the opposite direction!

The beautiful pinewoods along the **Col de Bavella** (1,243m) have alas not been spared some of the ravages of forest fires and other environmental damage, particularly that from picnickers. There are plenty of waste bins, which are presumably functional rather than decorative — though this fact does not seem to have occurred to some of the visitors! But this need not detract from the beauty and fascination of the **Aiguilles de Bavella**, which seem almost close enough to grasp — and the scents of the forest that waft on the breeze. One need only walk a short distance to get away from the crowds and enjoy the solitary peace of the mountains. One might even be lucky enough to catch a glimpse of a mouflon — a rare form of wild sheep.

There is a marvellous walk to the **Col de Finosa**, an hour and a half away to the south. The route actually forms part of the famous mountain path called the Grande Randonnée or GR20, which runs all the way across the island from Calenzana in the north-west to Conca in the south-east (between Solenzara and Porto-Vecchio — see route 3). It crosses the road at the top of the pass (going left just beyond the restaurant), and is marked by red-and-white posts. The path is not a difficult one: it first drops down to cross a stream called San Petru, and then climbs up the

Zonza

other side. Only the last section is steep, or rather forms zigzags up the mountainside. There is a magnificent view from the top across the mountains and down to the coast, where one can just make out the church tower at Ste Lucie de Porto-Vecchio.

The road is less twisty as it descends through pine and chestnut forests to **Zonza** (784m; population 1,000). This popular mountain resort clings precariously to the hillside among the trees. Some of the bus tours round the island include an overnight stop here, plus a visit to the nearby village of Quenza.

Quenza (805m) is visible to the trained eye from Zonza, nestling among the woodlands on the side of the valley. The steep valley in between forces the road to approach it in a wide loop (it is 7km from Zonza along the D420 road to Aullène). The village's ⌘ main place of interest is the lovely Romanesque chapel of St Mary. A foundation stone to the left of the side door gives its date as 1000, making it the oldest surviving church in Corsica. On the return journey there is a good view of the Aiguilles de Bavella.

Visitors approaching the region from the west along the D268 (see page 165ff) will be able to see the **Aiguilles de Bavella** from as far away as the pass above Ste Lucie-de-Tallano. On the approach to Zonza, the peaks appear to rise sheer out of the forest, forming a guard of honour above the village. If they are

Dramatic scenery around Zonza

hidden by cloud or haze, one might well consider following the usual circular route (Bavella—Solenzara—Porto-Vecchio—l'Ospédale) in the opposite direction. With luck, the view may be clearer later in the day.

Those interested in prehistoric sites are recommended to visit the museum at **Levie** (9½km south of Zonza along the D268), and the amazing archaeological sites of **Cucuruzzu** and **Capula** (see pages 155-6). For those interested in medieval art, the church at Levie contains a beautiful ivory statue of Christ. Of more literary interest is the Genoese-style house where the Corsican poet Ugo Peretti (1747–1838) was born.

The nearby village of **Carbini** is also worth a short extra trip. Situated 8km along the road south of Levie, it is the site of the beautiful fourteenth-century Romanesque church of St Jean or San Giovanni. The church has a marvellous decorated arch, and was the meeting place for the religious and political sect of the Giovannali. The church of San Quilico stands almost next door, with a 30m high free-standing bell tower in between.

It is 40km from **Zonza** to Porto-Vecchio along the D368 via l'Ospédale. The whole journey is through glorious forest scenery. The highest point along this part of the route is the **Col d'Illarata** (1,008m), 12km south-east of Zonza. Looking back,

Calacuccia

Scala di Santa Regina

Bonifacio

one has a final glimpse of the **Aiguilles de Bavella** (or a first glimpse if travelling northwards).

During the next 10km to l'Ospédale, the road passes close to the Punta di u Diamante (1,198m) and runs along the shore of a new reservoir. In between the two there is a signposted path leading to the **Cascade de Piscia di Gallo** — a 50m high waterfall that has eroded its way back along a deep trench. The water flow is naturally best in the early spring.

L'Ospédale (812m) is 19km north-west of Porto-Vecchio. It commands a wide panorama of the east coast, stretching south across the straits to the hills of Sardinia. As the road leaves the village, it passes an enormous boat-shaped rock on the right. For the next 12km the landscape is full of curious rock formations as the road descends through the beautiful **Forêt de l'Ospédale**. The hills and woodlands provide a cool break for natives and tourists alike who are tired of the heat on the coast. There are numerous footpaths through the forest, and occasional sightings of wild boar.

The road descends steeply through the forest, passing through numerous twists and hairpins; it has dropped to only 74m by the time it arrives at the turning for Araggiu (see page 153) at the **Col de Punticella**, 5km before Porto-Vecchio. It is now only a short step to the coast, where one may lie on the beach and dream of the beauties of Bavella.

11 PROPRIANO

Holiday Centre in the South-West

Propriano is situated on the south side of the Gulf of Valinco. It is the largest tourist resort in south-western Corsica, closely followed by Porto Pollo and Olmeto-Plage, both of which are also well supplied with hotels and camping facilities.

With a population of 3,500, Propriano is the only one of the three that can be called a town. It also has a harbour, with summer passenger services from Marseille and Toulon. But there is nothing of interest here apart from the tourist facilities. The buildings along the shore consist mostly of concrete hotels with steel balconies. The harbour includes a marvellous marina or *port de plaisance*, and handles exports of wine and other goods from the nearby region of Sartenais.

When the harbour was being dredged at the beginning of this century, several interesting discoveries were made showing that the bay had been used by the Greeks and Romans as an anchoring point for their ships. The Genoese built a settlement here in 1230, which was later destroyed by the Saracens. Sampiero Corso landed here in 1557 during his campaign to free Corsica from Genoa with the help of the French.

The bay has now been handed over entirely to tourism. The rocks and beaches along the shore are a paradise for all kinds of water sports — from bathing and swimming to diving and snorkelling, from sailing and windsurfing to speedboats and waterskiing. Onshore activities include tennis and minigolf, walking and horseriding. And there are some lovely excursions into the area around, combining beautiful scenery with sites of great historic and prehistoric interest.

Excursions from Propriano

Viggianello (6km)
The village can be reached along a small road that leaves the

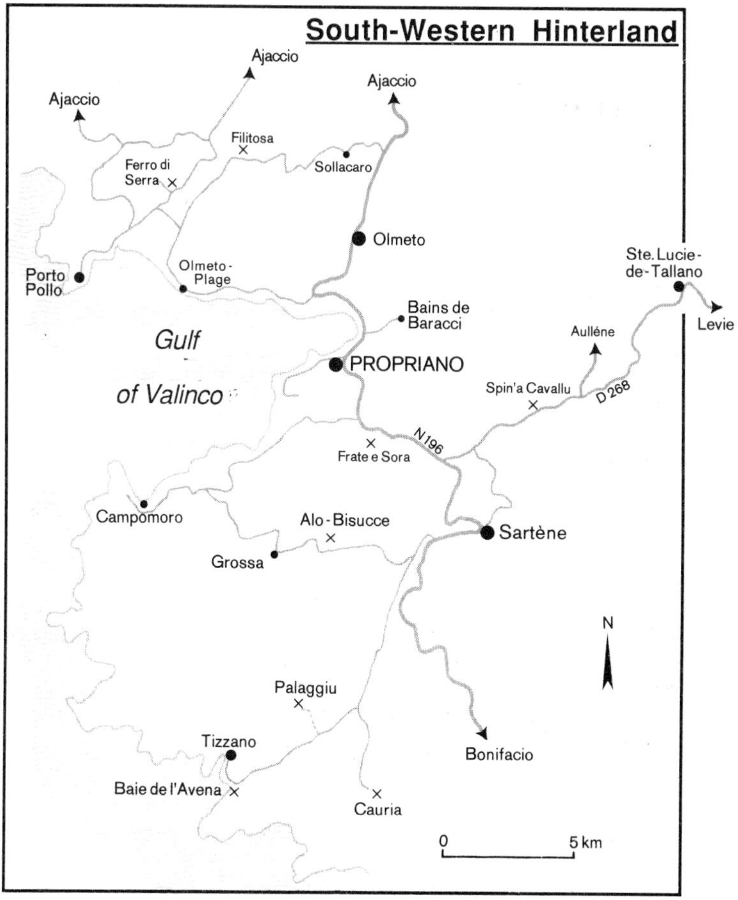

South-Western Hinterland

Ajaccio

Ajaccio

Ajaccio

Filitosa ×

Ferro di Serra ×

Sollacaro

● Olmeto

Ste. Lucie-
de-Tallano ●

Porto Pollo ●

Olmeto-
Plage ●

Bains de
● Baracci

Auléne

Levie

Gulf

● PROPRIANO

of Valinco

Spin'a Cavallu ×

D 268

N 196

Frate e Sora ×

Campomoro ●

Alo-Bisucce ×

● Sartène

Grossa ●

N

Palaggiu ×

Tizzano ●

Bonifacio

Baie de l'Avena ×

Cauria ×

0   5 km

N196 near the Col de Sta Giulia (see route 4), and probably provides one of the best views of the Gulf of Valinco. Also of interest
are the nearby sulphur baths known as the **Bains de Baraci**.

Campomoro (16km)

The route leaves the N196 Sartène road just south of the bridge
over the Rizzanèse, and runs along the south side of the bay past
several beaches and viewing points. The small fishing port of
Campomoro is rapidly developing into a tourist resort.

The beach at Propriano

Porto Pollo (20km)

Porto Pollo's beautiful coastal situation makes it a magnet for tourists in the summer. The route leaves the N196 north of Propriano at the point where it leaves the bay (see route 4). It follows the D157, passing above the series of interconnected beaches that make up the resort of **Olmeto-Plage**. The road turns inland to cross the River Taravo. Before the bridge there is a turning for **Filitosa** (see page 170), making an interesting detour on the way back to Propriano (27km). The road to Porto Pollo goes left over the bridge. Before arriving at Porto Pollo, it meets the coast road from Ajaccio (61km).

Ste Lucie-de-Tallano and Beyond

The route leaves the N196 about half-way to Sartène, and follows the D69 Aullène road along the course of the Rizzanèse. A short way further on, there is a path signposted to the thirteenth-century Genoese bridge of Spin'a Cavallu, which is hidden among the bushes to the left of the road.

![Ste Lucie de Tallano]

Ste Lucie de Tallano

The road continues along an avenue of eucalyptus trees, and soon comes to a fork. The D69 follows the left fork and continues through some beautiful scenery to Aullène (24km).

The present route goes right along the D268, which begins to climb steeply as it approaches **Ste Lucie-de-Tallano** (450m), which is about 21km from Propriano. The village clings to the hillside above the valley of the Rizzanèse. As the road approaches from below, it appears to be at the top of the hill. But this impression is soon dispelled as the higher slopes come into view.

Further up the hill to the left is the small village of **Sant'**

Andréa-di-Tallano, home of the famous Tallano wines. In clear weather there is a beautiful view from the top.

The main road continues to Levie (8½km), first climbing up the almost vertical slope to the right of Ste Lucie. At the first hairpin an old Franciscan monastery looms up out of the woods to the right. The sixteenth-century church contains a number of notable works of art. At the top of the pass is an old cemetery with a ruined chapel. Once the realm of the dead, the field is now used for playing football.

The road continues to climb for a little, then becomes level as it runs along a kind of balcony above a valley to the right. The tiny hamlet of **Mela** clings to a ridge above the valley, and the mountains of Bavella are visible in the distance. 3½km before **Levie**, there is a left turn signposted to the ancient Torrean sites of Castellu di Cucuruzzu and Capula (see page 155-6). Only 20km beyond Levie along the D268 is the famous mountain region of **Bavella** (see page 157ff).

Bonifacio (65km)
The route to Bonifacio follows the first part of route 4 in reverse. The place itself is described on page 175.

Sartène (13km)
With a population of 5,900, Sartène (305m) is the third-largest town on Corsica. It is 13km south-east of Propriano along the N196 Bonifacio road (see route 4). The town clings to the hillside above the valley of the Loreto. It is probably the most typically Corsican of all towns on the island, and almost seems to have been engraved on the landscape. This impression is further enhanced by the fact that many of the houses have been built on the bare rock, as is clearly visible at the entrance to the old town.

Visitors may stroll up and down through the steep, narrow lanes, passing under arches and washing lines full of clothes. Corners and windowsills are decorated with flowerpots, adding an extra splash of colour. Cats stalk their prey among the shadows, while dogs sleep soundly under the walls. The atmosphere is almost medieval, and the silence is broken only by the bustle of the market place or by the chatter of a busload of tourists.

It is difficult to imagine that Sartène was at one time a place of vendetta, where the nobility and the citizens of the town carried on a bitter war of revenge. It was also a centre of Corsican resistance in their struggle against Genoese oppression.

Sartène

At the centre of the town is the market place or Place de la Libération. A gateway leads to the left of the town hall into the maze of steps and alleyways that makes up the old town. The first turn along here to the left leads back to the main N196, and up to the watchtower that forms part of the sole surviving section of the twelfth-century fortifications. The citadel once towered over the town hall and the river beneath.

The main church stands next to the market place. Hanging up near the entrance are the cross and chain (*catena*) that are carried by the main protagonist in the famous Good Friday procession. Known as the Catenacciu, it is probably the best-known of Corsica's many religious ceremonies. *Catenacciu* is a Corsican word meaning the 'chained one' or 'penitent one'.

The procession begins at the main church, and carries on for 3 hours, going from church to church through the dark streets of the old town to the accompaniment of torches and lanterns. It represents the Stations of the Cross — the various stages leading up to the death of Christ. Eight 'penitents' dressed in black cloaks carry a statue of Christ on a bier with a black canopy. 'Simon of Cyrene' walks before them in a white cloak. In front of him is the *Catenacciu*, who represents Christ himself. Clothed completely in red, he is bowed down by the weight of the cross and drags a heavy chain tied round his right ankle.

The ceremony finishes back at the main church with an emotional sermon and a blessing. At this point the *Catenacciu* finds refuge and escapes unnoticed. The priest is the only one who knows the *Catenacciu's* identity. He was at one time a genuine penitent — often a bandit seeking atonement for his misdeeds. This may often still be the case today, since potential candidates must apply to the priest. There is a waiting list lasting several years, but candidates may only play the part once in a lifetime.

Also worth visiting is the Prehistoric Museum (Musée de Préhistoire Corse), which is signposted from the market place. It is situated somewhat higher up in the former *maison d'arrêt* (built in 1843). It is a carefully planned collection of exhibits and photographs from the archaeological sites in the region, giving vivid insights into life on ancient Corsica.

The sites themselves are probably even more interesting, providing as it were a doorway into the past (see below).

Excursions into the Past

The area around the Gulf of Valinco includes a number of fascinating prehistoric sites. They have revealed much about the development of the early Megalithic people, and also about their relations with the Torreans that followed them.

The Tizzano region to the south is equally interesting. Its many Middle and Late Stone Age sites are set in areas of great beauty, and are ideal material for a day trip from Propriano or other local resorts.

Castellu di Cucuruzzu and Capula (31km)

The route is given under **Ste Lucie-de-Tallano** (see page 164ff). The sites themselves are described on page 155-6.

The Tizzano Valley (30km)

The route goes south from Propriano along the N196 Bonifacio road (see route 4). The first item of archaeological interest is just past the bridge over the Rizzanèse. It is a pair of menhirs called the *Frate e Sora* ('Brother and Sister'), standing in a meadow to the right of the road. The Prehistoric Museum in Sartène is also worth visiting *en route* (see above).

The route leaves the N196 at the **Col d'Albitrina** (2¹/₂km beyond Sartène), where it goes right along the D48 for Tizzano

(17km). About 2km along this road, there is a right turn along the D21 to Grossa, which eventually meets the coast road between Propriano and Campomoro, making an interesting route back (see below).

The D48 continues along the course of the Loreto towards Tizzano. After another 8km there is a small road to the left signposted to **Cauria** (5¹/₂km) — an area full of Megalithic sites, ⌘ including two double rows of menhirs (alignments) and a dolmen. This road first crosses another river valley, then runs along a ridge and comes to a dead end at the foot of a hill called Punta Cauria.

Immediately by the car park is the *Alignement i Stantari* ⌘ together with part of an ancient wall. The *Alignement de Renaggiu* starts by a copse about 300m away at the end of a well-trodden path. The famous *Dolmen of Fontenaccia,* also known as the *Stazzona del Diavolo* ('Devil's Smithy'), is situated on raised ground about 200m to the right of the car park. It is without doubt the finest and best-preserved dolmen on the island. The seven vertical slabs are sunk about half a metre into the ground, rising to about head-height above it; they support a horizontal slab measuring 3.4m long by 2.9m across. There are two small menhirs nearby.

Returning to the D48, the route continues for another 2km towards Tizzano. There is a footpath to the right signposted to the *Alignements de Palaggiu* (1km). The site includes several double ⌘ rows of menhirs, amounting to about ninety in all. Three of them have been made into stone statues on which weapons are depicted. This indicates that they belong to the final phase of the Megalithic culture (around 1500 BC), when the Torreans were beginning to take over the island.

The landscape is mostly heath-like in character, with sandy soils partly covered in *maquis.* The presence of fences shows that it is used for grazing goats. Irrigation is needed here to produce any wine or fruit. The undulating terrain is dotted with low, craggy summits with *tafoni* formations.

It is only another 3km from Palaggiu to the sea. The D48 runs along a sandy beach on the Baie d'Avena to the village of **Tizzano**, where the coast is more rocky. There are several restaurants here, and an old Genoese tower on a nearby headland.

The route returns along the D48 towards Sartène — that is, as far as the D21 junction (see above). There is another interesting

The Alignements de Palaggiu

site about 5km along the D21, just past the Bocca di Biscelli. On a
hill behind a farmhouse to the right are the remains of a Torrean
fortification called **Alo-Bisucce**. To get there one must scram-
ble through the bushes, there being no path as yet, though plans
are afoot to create one.

Archaeological investigations have unearthed a large number
of Megalithic remains. The Torreans must therefore have taken
over the original Megalithic complex and converted it for their own
purposes. They built a tower temple at the top of the hill, which,
though unremarkable from the outside, has some interesting
internal features. The vaulting has collapsed to reveal four small
passages going off the inner chamber, each bending sharply to
create a kind of swastika pattern.

It goes without saying that there are some good views from
here. It is now only another 10km to the south coast of the Gulf of
Valinco, along which one may return to Propriano.

Filitosa (18–21km)
The Filitosa site is by the D57, 9km east of the N196 Ajaccio road
(see route 4), and 4km north of the D157 Porto Pollo road. Both

Filitosa

approach routes are well-signposted.

Filitosa is without doubt the most important prehistoric site on Corsica, and appears to have been the main creative centre of the island's ancient Megalithic culture. It was here that the Megalithic artists reached the pinnacle of their achievement, albeit partly under the influence of the Torreans who settled nearby.

The newly-arrived Bronze Age Torreans first lived peaceably in the south-east of the island. But later they began to advance across the island, ousting the Megalithic inhabitants of the south-west. In 1400 BC they drove them out of Filitosa and built their own fortification on the site. Thus all the visible structures at Filitosa are Torrean in origin.

Much has also been found here from other periods, including pottery going back to the beginning of the New Stone Age (about 6000 BC), and items from later periods right down to the Middle Ages. Examples of these are shown in the museum to the right of the site entrance. But such material is secondary in comparison to the Megalithic menhirs and statues that have made Filitosa so famous.

One of the key exhibits is by the left-hand wall in the main part of the museum. It is a restored menhir known as *Scasa Murta*, the top half of which was discovered in the Taravo Valley below the main site. This Megalithic representation of a Torrean warrior reveals certain features that identify the Torreans as a seafaring race: holes in the helmet with horns coming out of them, a breastplate and a sword belt. Attempts have been made to link them with another Mediterranean race called the Shardans, and even with the earliest Vikings!

Another of the exhibits is *Filitosa XII* — a menhir that the Torreans split up for their own use, but which has now been reconstructed to something like its original form. It is one of the few examples with arm extensions, showing the transition from a carved stone to a statue. On the right is an earlier example called *Tappa II*, which is much less like a statue — an indication of the problems that these Stone Age sculptors had to overcome.

Yet another key exhibit is *Filitosa V*, which has been erected half-way along the path going up to the ancient cemetery. It depicts a bronze longsword and a dagger in a sheath. Both are of a kind that was usual elsewhere in the Mediterranean, but which was never used by the Megalithic people on Corsica. The top part is missing, but is thought to have represented a face — hence its nickname the 'Watchman'. It is 3m high and weighs two tonnes, making it the second-largest menhir on the island.

The Torrean fortification is at the top of the hill, and measures 130m by 40m. The entrance is at the eastern end, where some of the massive stone walls still remain that originally circled it. Immediately to the right of the entrance is a sloping area known as the eastern complex, where naturally-occurring rocks have been incorporated into the wall structures. House foundations have also been found on the bare rock to the left.

The tower temple is in the middle of the site. Its walls and foundations include pieces of menhirs that the Torreans used for stone, with total disregard for the Megalithic people that had created them. Some of them have been dug up by archaeologists and placed on top of the tower.

The top sections of six menhir statues have been placed in higher positions either side of the passage leading to the temple chamber. They were given the names *Filitosa VIII, XI* and *VII* (on the left), *IX, X* and *XIII* (on the right). *Filitosa VIII* is like *Scasa Murta* in having a sword belt, while *Filitosa VIII* and *XIII* both appear to be wearing armour at the back. The face depicted on *Filitosa IX* is thought to represent the climax of Megalithic sculpture on Corsica, and is considered one of the great masterpieces of Megalithic culture in Europe generally.

To the right of the entrance is a polished stone with two depressions in it, which is presumed to have served some other purpose before being used as a building stone. In the temple chamber itself there were traces of burning on the hard earth floor; there were also the remains of an altar and a drainage channel, indicating some form of sacrificial rite. The vaulted stone ceiling has as usual fallen in.

Behind the tower temple, also known as the central complex, there are further menhir fragments belonging to *Filitosa VI*, which appears to be wearing a longsword and armour like *Filitosa IX*. It is labelled *XV*, but this number refers to its position on the site. Further down the hillside to the left, some of the outer wall belonging to the original Megalithic site has been uncovered.

At the top of the hill is an enormous rock marking the western end of the hill-top fortress. There is a passage to the right of it leading down to a temple outside the fortification walls. Known as the western complex, it was undoubtedly added later, when the Torreans had gained a firm foothold at Filitosa and no longer feared attacks from their enemies.

For some reason the Torreans closed off the forward part of the temple chamber, filling it with rubble and then walling it off (though it has now been cleared). Traces of burning have been found both here and in the chamber behind, indicating the practice of making burnt offerings. The traces in the back chamber have been dated to 1200 BC. A skull has also been found here. The ceiling has again fallen in.

Five more menhirs have been erected down in the valley. They stand beneath a spreading olive tree on the opposite bank of a stream bed, usually dried up, with cattle grazing peaceably around them. They were discovered on farmland surrounding the hill, which suggests that they were in some way connected with the Megalithic temple site on the hill top. They have been given the following names: (from left to right) *Filitosa III* and *IV*, each with a dagger; *Filitosa I*, with a diagonal sword; *Tappa I*, on which the neck and the back of the head are clearly depicted; and a highly eroded menhir, *Filitosa II*.

Looking back up the hill, there is a good view of the whole of the Filitosa site, part of it considerably overgrown. The colours are particularly good towards sunset.

Serra-di-Ferro (15km)

This site is only 5½km from Filitosa, just off the D157 coast road to Porto Pollo. It is a short way beyond the bridge over the Taravo along the small side-road to Pietra Rossa.

⌘   A dolmen and a menhir are visible to the right of the road, just past the hamlet of Favellelo. The menhir is called the *Paladin*; it is 2.9m high and weighs 1½ tonnes. The path to the dolmen on the hill goes past two more menhirs. They are 2.25m and 3m high respectively, but are half buried in the ground. The dolmen is only small, measuring 1.2m in height; it has clearly been built out of the local red-coloured stone.

12 BONIFACIO

Corsica's Southernmost Point

Bonifacio is considered by many to be the most delightful little town on the whole island. It looks particularly lovely from the sea — which is one reason among many for making the short trip to Sardinia.

The southern point of Corsica emerges dream-like from the haze like a kind of mirage. As one approaches from Sardinia, the details of the chalk cliffs become clearer. The old fortified town can be seen, perched on the edge of the cliff, 60m above the sea. One searches for the harbour — but in vain. The only way in seems to be a flight of steps cut into the side of the cliff.

These are supposed to have been the work of troops of the king of Aragon, who hacked them out of the chalk in one night during the siege of 1421. This does not seem to have helped them to capture Bonifacio. For the beleaguered citizens, in a final desperate bid for freedom, tipped the last of their food supplies onto the besieging troops from above. The ploy seems to have worked, because the Spaniards withdrew in disarray. According to another theory, the citizens made the staircase themselves for bringing in supplies from overseas when the harbour was blockaded.

The boat from Sardinia appears to be making straight for the cliff face. It is some time before a gap opens up in the cliff through which the boat then steers. There is a small lighthouse to the left of it and a cave to the right. One can see clearly how the sea has eroded the cliffs from below, creating an overhang that could easily break off and crash into the sea together with the houses on top of it. The boat turns sharply to the right, and runs along a narrow inlet parallel to the sea. As it enters the harbour the scene suddenly changes, and it feels as though one has been transplanted to the French Riviera.

The road approach is in many ways equally surprising. As one comes in across a uniform chalk plateau, one little imagines that the valley will suddenly open out into a beautiful landlocked harbour, with a citadel straddling the headland above it.

The newer part of the town is down by the harbour. It still has an old-fashioned air, with its little shops and hotels and brightly-coloured sunshades. The harbour front accommodates a bus terminus, various car- and boat-hire firms, and several tour operators offering trips to local caves and islands. Hundreds of little boats bob gently on the quiet blue waters of the harbour.

To the right of the harbour front is a small church dedicated to St Erasmus. To the left of it is a path with steps leading up to the **Chapelle St Roch** — the seamen's church, built on the site where Bonifacio's last plague victim died in 1528. From here there is a marvellous view across the sea, and also down to a small gravelly beach at the bottom of the cliff. The chapel stands on a neck of land where the cliff is lower. To the left is the southern headland of Capo Pertusato, while the old fortified town towers up on the cliffs to the right.

Pedestrians may walk up along an old cobbled path that crosses where the old drawbridge once was and enters via the old city gate or **Porta Vecchia**. The road, which has come up via a longer route from the closed end of the harbour, follows a gentler course, running in a loop above the harbour and entering the old town via a newer gate called the **Porte-Neuve**.

The main street in the old town is the Rue Scamaroni, which is the only street where traffic is allowed. The other lanes and alleyways are too narrow and are often broken up by steps.

Bonifacio today has a population of only 2,100. It was founded in 830, when a Tuscan margrave called Bonifatius built a small fortification here to repel Saracen attacks. One large tower remains from this period. In 1195, during the struggles between Pisa and Genoa, Bonifacio was captured by the Genoese in a surprise attack. In order to be sure of keeping the fortress, they installed some of Genoa's most loyal citizens, and granted them a variety of special privileges, including the right to mint their own coinage.

Bonifacio grew into a powerful garrison town, and was only once captured by hostile forces. This was when Sampiero Corso took it for a short time in the sixteenth century. Otherwise it has remained impregnable, even to Pasquale Paoli's Corsican nationalists — a factor which Napoléon Bonaparte used to advantage when he held Bonifacio for the French.

Visitors strolling through the old town will find an atmosphere of peace and timelessness. Though full of little narrow streets, it is

Bonifacio

impossible to get lost in. Behind the lines of washing, the old family crests are still visible on the fronts of the houses — that of the Doria family, for instance, with a lion rampant holding a ring in its paw. None of the old houses have living quarters on the ground floor — another relic from the past. The doors leading to staircases are a modern adaptation. Originally the ground floor was walled in, and one would have entered via a rope ladder to the first floor, which could be pulled up at times of danger.

The suggested tour of the old town leaves the Rue Scamaroni along the Rue Longue, which is reached via a flight of stone steps leading up from opposite the post office. Two famous buildings stand opposite each other at the top of the steps. To the left is the house where Napoléon lived when he was the officer in charge of the Bonifacio garrison in 1793. To the right is the house where Charles V of Austria stayed in 1541 during his return from Algiers, when bad weather forced him to shelter his fleet in the nearby Gulf of Sta Manza.

The Rue Longue comes out into a small square, to the right of which is the old city gate or **Porta Vecchia**, built in 1598. It still retains its old wooden doors, but the drawbridge on the other side has been replaced by a stone bridge called the **Pont Levis**. A cobbled path comes across it from the Chapelle St Roch (see above).

The route follows a small cobbled street that goes south from the square along the inside of the battlements. It passes a lookout point on the left called the Belvédère de Manichella. A little further along, the route bears left down the Rue de Gaulle.

To the right of the Rue de Gaulle is Bonifacio's most important church, **Ste Marie-Majeur**. This triple-naved structure was built in the twelfth century during the period of Pisan rule. The Genoese made several alterations, adding a number of Gothic features. There is a fountain under the loggia that collects rainwater from the roof via the buttresses. There are many more of these ingenious drainage channels in other parts of the old town.

The most interesting feature inside the church is a third-century pre-Christian sarcophagus, which stands beneath a beautifully carved fifteenth-century marble tabernacle. The vestry contains a much-treasured relic, reputedly a piece of Christ's cross. It is carefully preserved, and is processed through the streets on special occasions. The most important of these is the Good Friday procession, which is instituted by the five fraternities of Bonifacio.

The Rue de Gaulle continues downhill past the **Chapel of John the Baptist**, and eventually meets the Rue Scamaroni coming up from the right. The route now turns left along the Rue St Dominique, which leads to the church of the same name and the **citadel**. The citadel is occupied by the foreign legion, and is officially a military zone. Visitors may not enter the church or the citadel unless accompanied by an official guide.

St Dominic's Church is situated by the entrance to the citadel. Its most striking feature is the octagonal bell tower with its cluster of small spires. The typically Gothic buttresses that run round the outside are one of the features that make it Corsica's only substantially Gothic church. The original structure, however, goes back much earlier. It was founded in 1270 by the Knights Templar on the site of an eighth- or ninth-century church, as is indicated by certain bas-relief designs in the foundations. In the fourteenth century it was extended by the Dominicans. It contains many beautiful treasures, including the eighteenth-century main altar, made of white marble with different-coloured stone decorations.

The cemetery is situated further out along the headland. It is full of typically Corsican family mausoleums, many of which have fallen into disrepair. **St Francis' Chapel** is close by. It was part of a now ruined monastery, built to commemorate St Francis' visit to Bonifacio. Not far away is **Bartholomew's Well** — a 65m deep shaft, which was sunk in the eighteenth century. In order to draw water from it, a spiral flight of steps was cut out of the side of the shaft leading down to the bottom.

Excursions from Bonifacio

Capo Pertusato (4km)
Capo Pertusato is the most southerly point of the Corsican mainland. It is possible to drive almost all the way to the lighthouse at the point. The route leaves the town along the D58 Santa Manza road, and immediately turns right along a side-road signposted to the lighthouse.

One can also walk there along a path that goes left from the Chapelle St Roch. It runs along the top of the cliff past a semaphore station to the lighthouse. This is not advisable in a strong wind or in the heat of the day in summer, since the path runs over treeless terrain and close to a dangerous cliff.

The cape provides some marvellous views across the sea to Sardinia and the islands to the east, and also back to Bonifacio and the mainland.

The Gulf of Santa Manza (6–8km)
The route leaves Bonifacio along the D58, which crosses to the end of the inlet and runs for a short distance along its southern shore. The bay has some marvellous beaches between areas of rock. It is a good if somewhat inaccessible area for bathing and aquatic sports.

On the way the road passes the old convent of St Julien, which was built in the twelfth or thirteenth century and includes certain Gothic features. Shortly after it there is a right turn to a beach and viewing point called Calalonga Plage.

L'Ermitage de la Trinité (8km)
The route leaves Bonifacio along the N196 Sartène road, and turns left along a small side-road just before the Bocca d'Arbia

(138m). The 'hermitage' is prettily situated to the right of the road. The simple little chapel is built of white chalk.

About half an hour's walk away is the Cap de Feno, with its semaphore station and lighthouse. The view makes it well worth the effort.

Boat Trips from Bonifacio

There are numerous boat excursions to the many caves and grottos along the coast around Bonifacio. It is worth noting, however, that they can only run when the sea is fairly calm. The most famous is the **Grotte du Sdragonato** to the west of Bonifacio. The roof of this cave has a hole in the shape of Corsica. It can also be reached on foot along a path that goes past the lighthouse opposite the harbour entrance. To the east of Bonifacio is **St Anthony's Grotto**, which has some beautiful stalactites.

The Lavezzi Islands

Visitors with more time are recommended to try the somewhat longer trip to this group of granite islands to the east. In 1855 a frigate went down here with all hands, killing 773 men. The corpses which were recovered were buried in two graveyards on the main island, one of which has a small chapel. A pyramid-shaped monument was erected on a nearby reef.

A short distance to the north are the island of **Cavallo** and its tiny granite neighbour **San Bainzo**, which has been quarried for building stone since the time of the Romans. A granite block from here was used for the war memorial in Bonifacio, which stands next to the road between the lower and upper town (see above). Cavallo has a strange row of rough-hewn stone columns from the third or fourth century AD.

Sardinia

A visit to Sardinia is not to be missed. It is only an hour away on the ferry from Bonifacio to Sta Teresa. The port and seaside resort of **Sta Teresa** lies high up on the cliff above an inlet. It offers more than just a nice little beach. When the water level is low, rock climbers may care to make a short expedition down the cliffside to the **Isola d'Amore** — an island of sheer cliffs that can be reached via a series of rocks.

The cliffs at the nearby **Capo Testa** are even more

breathtaking by comparison. Situated 5km west of Sta Teresa, it is accessible by bus and has restaurant facilities. There are several small bathing beaches and opportunities for swimming around the rocks. In two places the remains of some old Roman columns can be seen. Visitors should follow the road as far as it goes and continue through a gate in a fence saying 'Entry forbidden — military zone'. There is a small path to the right leading to some quite astonishing cliff formations.

Visitors to Sardinia from Corsica may note the striking similarity of the spoken dialects either side of the straits. This also explains why the north Corsicans think that the south Corsicans speak Sardinian!

13 ADVICE TO TOURISTS

1. Planning the Journey

The information given in this chapter is subject to change without notice and is for general guidance only. Up-to-date information is always available from the French Government Tourist Office or travel agents.

For those who prefer to have everything planned for them, there is a wide choice of different package holidays available. Details of these can be obtained from travel agents.

People who wish to travel under their own steam should contact an automobile association or travel agent to find out all the most up-to-date information about the bookings and documents required. It is vital to book air, train and ferry reservations well in advance, especially when travelling in the high season.

How to Get There

There are several different ways of travelling to Corsica

Travelling by Air
There are regular air flights from Paris, Nice and Marseille in France to Ajaccio, Bastia, Figari and Calvi on Corsica, with connecting services from airports in Britain and the USA. Charter and package-tour organisations provide non-stop flights from Britain.

Travelling by Ferry
All the ferry routes from France are run by the SNCM (*Société Nationale Maritime Corse-Méditerranée*). There are services from Marseille, Toulon and Nice to Bastia, Ile Rousse, Calvi, Ajaccio and Propriano.

At least two operators run ferries from Italy: Corsica Ferries operate from Genoa, La Spezia and Livorno (Leghorn) to Bastia, and from San Remo (near the French border) to Bastia and Calvi; NAV.AR.MA operates between Piombino and Bastia.

All ferries carry cars (regulations must be strictly observed), and all ports are served by railways, including a number of useful car-rail services.

Passport and Driving Licence
An ordinary passport is quite sufficient for British holidaymakers entering France or passing through Switzerland and Italy *en route*. A full British or US driving licence is also sufficient for driving in these countries. However, it is important to check up on all regulations beforehand with an automobile association or travel agent. *Non-EEC visitors now require a visa.* Your nearest French consulate will answer queries on visas. US citizens could contact one of the Department of State Passport Agencies, major post offices or some courthouses.

Health and Insurance
All holidaymakers should enquire at their local health centre or social security office regarding reciprocal health arrangements. At all events, health and luggage insurance is advisable, and can often be arranged in conjunction with travel bookings. Car drivers are advised to take out extra insurance to cover any necessary emergency repairs.

Health care in Corsica is very good on the whole, while pharmacists have a good supply of medicines. However, visitors who are accustomed to taking certain remedies for routine ailments should take a sufficient supply of these with them. It is also worth asking the advice of one's own doctor.

Clothing
It is worth remembering to take at least one warm pullover. Even in the hottest of summers it can be cool in the evenings or up in the mountains. Trousers are considered more suitable than shorts away from the beach. Visitors who wish to dine out in the evenings should take something smarter for the occasion.

Three swimsuits are always better than two; one swimsuit is never enough, unless one wishes to risk catching cold by running around in damp swimwear. Beach shoes or trainers can be as essential on stony beaches as stout boots are for walking in the mountains. It is also wise to take a light raincoat, especially in the spring or autumn.

Customs Regulations
A visitor from an EEC country over 17 years of age may take the

following amounts of goods into France (Corsica): 300 cigarettes or 150 cigarillos or 75 cigars or 400g tobacco; 1.5 litres drinks over 38.8 per cent proof or 3 litres not over 38.8 per cent proof plus 5 litres of still table wine; 1000g coffee or 400g coffee extract; 200g tea or 80g tea extract; 75g perfume; 0.375 litres eau de cologne; other goods such as souvenirs up to a value of 2,400F (620F/person under 15). (Allowance is given for equivalent combinations of items such as spirits and wine, etc.) Visitors from non-EEC countries are entitled to: 200 cigarettes, 100 cigarillos, 50 cigars or 250g tobacco; 2 litres table wine and either 1 litre of drinks over 38.8 per cent proof or 2 litres of drinks under 38.8 per cent proof; 50g perfume; 500g coffee, 200g coffee extract, 40g tea or extract and other goods up to a value of 300F (150F for children under 15).

Other Things to Remember
Although camera films and cosmetics are in plentiful supply on Corsica, they are often expensive, so it is worth taking a good supply from home. Car drivers should take a repair kit in case of need.

2. Travelling on Corsica

Information about roads and transport on Corsica is available beforehand from automobile associations; from travel agents or from hotel and camping organisations. The French Government Tourist Office also provides ample information.

It is also possible to make further enquiries on arrival at the local tourist information office (*Syndicat d'Initiative*) or town hall (*mairie*). Most hotels provide local details and advise on possible tours and excursions.

Maps
The best map of Corsica is No. 90 in the Michelin series, which was used in the preparation of this book. More detailed maps of different parts of the island can be obtained on arrival in Corsica.

The island has recently been resurveyed, with the result that there may be discrepancies of up to 20m in some of the spot heights given. Note also that the road system is still being improved, and the most recent changes may not have been recorded on even the most up-to-date maps. In such cases it is important to pay attention to road signs.

Place names are rendered variously in French, Italian and Corsican, and the Corsican spelling is often inconsistent. But the differences are fortunately small, so there is no problem in understanding what is meant.

Car Driving

The first commandment for all car drivers on Corsica is *take care*! The main roads are mostly well made, and are being continually further improved. But the mountainous terrain inevitably makes them twisty, and they are narrow in places too. Not for nothing has Corsica been called the land of the 100,000 bends! However, the roads are usually well-signposted.

Drivers should stay on the right-hand side of the road, drive gently and sound the horn at blind corners. It is not just other vehicles that sometimes block the way. Corsica has a large population of donkeys and other animals that have discovered the pleasures of walking on the road. Hooting does not always help in such cases!

Drivers should always have a spare can of fuel in case of emergencies, and fill up at every opportunity. Many filling stations are closed on Sundays and at lunch times.

Vehicles for Hire

The island's many car hire firms offer a wide choice of vehicles for the purposes of exploring the island. It is also possible to book hire-cars and caravans in advance. Some firms also offer motor bikes and mopeds for hire.

Taxis are available all over Corsica, but only those in the towns are metered. If a taxi is not metered, it is advisable to agree on a price beforehand.

Railways

There are effectively only two lines in Corsica, and these only offer a full service in the high season. The main route runs through the mountains from Ajaccio via Ponte Leccia to Bastia, with a branch going off from Ponte Leccia to Ile Rousse and Calvi. Each route has one train a day in both directions, with additional local services along the north-west coast between Calvi and Ile Rousse.

Buses and Coaches

The bus is the main means of transport on the island. But there are no more than one or two buses a day on most of the routes.

The French railways or SNCF (*Société Nationale des Chemins de Fer*) offer a special *Service Touristique* — a six-day luxury coach service that goes all the way round the island. One can either go the whole way round, stopping overnight (or longer) at the end of each stage, or else one can just travel along individual sections of the route, such as Calvi to Bastia via Cap Corse, or Bonifacio to Corte stopping at Ghisoni for lunch. The service runs at least twice a week in both directions.

There are numerous possibilities for whole-day or half-day excursions, organised by the SNCF and other local organisations.

Ferries

The ferries from Bastia to Elba and from Bonifacio to Sardinia are effectively local services, and can be used for day excursions.

Air Transport

Local flights run between Ajaccio, Bastia, Calvi, Propriano and Bonifacio/Figari. Air-taxi services are also provided between these same airports.

3. Accommodation

Hotel and other accommodation is good and plentiful on Corsica. The only problems might be in popular resorts during the high season in July and August. It is always advisable to book accommodation in advance, at least for the first or major 'ports of call'. Other bookings can then be made as time and opportunity allow.

Accommodation in Corsica tends to be simple and unpretentious, even somewhat basic. The French Government Tourist Office provides a full list of what is available, including rented and chalet accommodation. Details of nudist camping sites and holiday villages are also provided.

In general the west coast, with its rocks and inlets, is more exclusive and therefore dearer. The east coast, with almost 100km of beach, is cheaper and more popular. Accommodation inland is without doubt the cheapest of all. Visitors outside the high season enjoy reductions of between 10 per cent and 20 per cent.

Campsite, Bavella region

Camping

Camping is very popular on Corsica, and there are plenty of good camping sites all over the island. They are often linked to restaurant and sporting facilities. Some sites provide tents and caravans for hire, so that campers need not take large amounts of equipment with them.

Camping is now forbidden outside officially designated sites, since local authorities no longer provide permits. The reason for this is the enormous fire risk in areas of forest and *maquis.* It is much easier to start a bush fire than anyone could possibly imagine, and the result is potentially disastrous for both human and animal alike, indeed for the whole ecology of the island. **Everyone must therefore take extreme care with any form of fire whatsoever**.

4. Food and Drink

The most distinctive feature of Corsican cuisine is the skilful blending of the many different herbs that grow in the Corsican mountains — thyme, mint, basil, fennel, aniseed, sage, borage, rosemary, myrtle, marjoram and juniper, to name but a few. The Corsicans also use a lot of mushrooms and other edible fungi.

Glossary of Terms Found on Menus

Casse-croûte: any sort of snack

Starters
Charcuterie corse: smoked sausages and other cooked meats
Oursins: sea-urchins (the best in the world!)
Pâté de merle: blackbird pâté seasoned with myrtle

Main Courses
Bastelle: leek, broccoli, parsley and borage leaves, softened in olive oil and baked in bread-dough
Bianchetti: whitebait — tiny fish dipped in batter and deep-fried in olive oil
Caprettu: roast kid
Caprettu a l'istrettu: ragout of kid, highly seasoned
Coppa: pork shoulder smoked with herbs
Formaiu di porcu: brawn seasoned with onion, pepper and herbs
Langoustes à la Corse: lobsters (the best in the Mediterranean!)

in a piquant sauce prepared from the stock with olive oil, wine
vinegar, pepper, salt, etc

Lonzu: smoked fillet of pork

Migisca: smoked fillet of goat

Pivarunata: a kind of paprika stew

Rifreda: lamb roasted on a spit; also lamb's or kid's liver or
tongue in a highly seasoned sauce

Tianu de Cignale: wild boar hotpot with onions, garlic and
potatoes

Tianu di fave: ragout of pork with haricot beans

Tianu di Pisi: a hotpot made with onions, carrots, peas and pieces
of grilled bacon

Stuffatu: braised blackbird, kid or lamb with pasta and sprinkled
with finely grated hard cheese

Suppa corsa: a vegetable soup rather like Italian minestrone

Tripette: well-seasoned tripe

Ziminu: bouillabaisse — fish soup with croûtons and sprinkled
with finely grated hard cheese

Desserts

Brocciu: a kind of cream cheese made from goat's milk and eaten
with fruit or figs (also used with peppermint in a kind of
omelette)

Cocciula; *fiadonu*; *imbrocciatta*: fritters with *brocciu* in the
batter and flavoured with brandy, rum or lemon juice

Cakes and Biscuits

Fritelli; *pisticcini*: doughnuts made with chestnut flour

Burlamondi; *frappi*: puff pastries

Canestre; *canestrelli*; *canestroni*: cakes made with flour, eggs
and butter

Cacavelli: large *canestroni* with hard-boiled eggs in the middle
(popular at Easter time)

Corsican Wines

Corsica's wines have a distinctive aroma of their own that reminds
one of the *maquis*. The red wines have a lovely deep red colour
and an excellent flavour. The white wines are full-flavoured but
not heavy. The most popular sweet wines (muscatels and
malvasias) are those of Cap Corse, Piana and Porto. Rosé from
Cap Corse is the most usual with meals. The local country wines
make adequate house wines for self-catering purposes.

Aperitifs, Liqueurs and Spirits

These are mostly flavoured with herbs from the *maquis*, giving them a distinctively Corsican taste. *Cédratine* is a liqueur made from citrons. *Marc* and *Aquavita* are forms of brandy. *Pastis* is made from aniseed, and is better known under the trade name *Pernod*. It is usually diluted with water, which gives it a milky yellow colour. It can also be mixed with mint or almond liqueur.

5. Sport

The Corsicans seem to prefer to leave most sporting activities to their guests. They have no interest in skiing or other mountain pursuits. They sometimes go sailing, swimming or riding — and love watching football, having one or two stars of their own. But their favourite is the French game of *boules*, which they play with carefully exaggerated enthusiasm. They are, however, keen to encourage their guests to play sports, if only for commercial reasons.

Water Sports

The coastal resorts provide ample facilities for every kind of water sport. There are all kinds of boats for hire, from paddle and rowing boats to speedboats.

Yachting is popular, with a large number of clubs around the coast. There are regattas throughout the summer, with participants from both home and abroad. There are yachts for hire at Ajaccio, Bastia, Calvi, Ile Rousse, Sant' Ambroggio and St Florent. The sailing school at St Florent provides courses for beginners.

Water skiing and windsurfing are both extremely popular; private courses are available at many resorts, and there are special training schools at Calvi and St Florent.

Swimming and bathing require few special facilities. The east coast is almost a continuous beach. The small bays along the west coast are not always sandy, but are quieter and more private. Cap Corse in particular provides some idyllic bathing spots in the tiny coves along the coast. The more popular beaches provide sunshades and deckchairs for hire, together with changing and shower facilities.

Snorkelling has become almost commonplace along the rocky

Watersports in a Tizzano bay

western shores, and is not difficult to learn. Diving, on the other hand, requires considerably more training and equipment. Divers are advised to seek assistance from experts with local knowledge of the coast. This point applies in particular to participants in the increasingly popular activity of underwater treasure hunting. Cap Corse is again the most popular area, followed by the bays along the west coast — Calvi, Galeria, Tiuccia, Ajaccio, Porto Pollo, Tizzano, Figari — and the Gulfs of Porto-Vecchio and Sta Manza in the south-east.

Hunting and Fishing

Angling is popular in the rivers and streams in the mountains, where the local trout or *fario* is a special attraction. It is also abundant in the high mountain lakes, though camping equipment is needed for venturing this far. The main fishing season is from March to June. Freshwater eels can be caught all the year round, and can be found in all streams up to 400m above sea level.

Those who wish to go sea fishing should try to make friends with local fishermen. The waters around Corsica support as many as 200 species of sea fish, of which some at least are bound to take the bait. The reward for one's efforts may well be a tasty fish soup (see **Food and Drink** above).

Hunting is a sport in which visitors rarely participate. But guests are nonetheless very much welcomed by local hunting parties. The best places for hunting are the areas around Evisa, Levie, Olmeto and Portinello.

Wild boar hunts are especially popular in all the *maquis* regions. The boar-hunting season is from early September to 1 January. The hunts are often organised by local hotel proprietors, who will always be helpful with advice. Mouflon, on the other hand, are a protected species, and must not be hunted.

The season for small game such as partridge, quail, blackbird, thrush, pigeon and hare is from late August to early January. The wetlands and lagoons along the east coast support large populations of species such as mallard, scoter, snipe and lapwing, all of which may be hunted from early July to mid-February. The wild goose season, on the other hand, is from 15 November to 31 March.

Hill-Walking and Climbing
The mountains of Corsica provide ample opportunities for both these activities. New footpaths are continually being marked out, while huts and refuges are springing up all over the place.

Experienced climbers usually go for the highest peaks. Monte Cinto can be climbed from Asco or from Calacuccia, Paglia Orba and Capo Tafonato from the Col de Vergio, Monte Rotondo from Corte, Monte d'Oro from Vizzavona, Monte Renoso from Bastelica or the Col de Verde, and Monte Incudine from Zicavo.

The longest mountain path is the famous Grande Randonnée or GR20, which runs all the way through the national park from Calenzana in Balagne in the north-west to Conca near Ste Lucie de Porto-Vecchio in the south-east. It is marked by red-and-white posts, and self-catering and emergency accommodation is provided in places along the route. There are also numerous shorter and easier routes for the ordinary visitor for whom the Corsican mountains are an essential part of the holiday.

Winter Sports
It may seem incredible that a Mediterranean island should provide

facilities for winter sports. But this is nonetheless true — and Corsica is particularly attractive in providing opportunities for mixing both summer and winter pursuits.

Areas above 1,400m can provide good snow conditions from December right into April. Corsica at present has two winter sports centres providing hotel and skiing facilities — *Castellucio* on the Col de Vergio and *Haut-Asco* on the Stagno Plateau. Skiing equipment can also be hired on the spot. Moves are afoot to create a cross-country skiing route along the GR20.

Other Sports
There are good riding facilities available for the small but increasing number of people wishing to explore the island on horseback. The Corsican riding clubs organise long tours, and welcome the opportunity to provide facilities for small private parties.

Tennis is yet another sport for which ample facilities are available at most hotels and resorts.

Further Information
More details of these and other sporting facilities are provided in an information leaflet published by the French Government Tourist Office, and also from certain travel agents.

6. Tips for Travellers

Souvenirs
The recent efforts to put Corsica on the tourist map have resulted in a revival of traditional Corsican crafts. A company called Corsicada has been set up for the express purpose of encouraging this trend. The company buys material from local artists and craftsmen and distributes it to recognised craft shops all over the island. Most of the goods carry the label *Casa di l'Artigiani*, which is a guarantee of quality.

The goods available include pottery, embroidery, basketwork and woodwork, and also wrought-iron, enamel and mosaic work. The beautiful decorative work includes coral brooches and *art galtique* — imaginative pictures made out of pebbles or small pieces of wood. These are sometimes more fun for the artist than the buyer, because taste is such an individual thing. So some visitors may care to buy the materials and create their own designs. Records of Corsican folk music are also recommended.

Food items for sale include jars of Corsican honey and boxes of candied citron. Another good souvenir is a bottle of myrtle or citron liqueur (*cédratine*), or a good wine from Cap Corse.

Opening Times

Shops are normally open Tuesdays to Saturdays 9am-12 noon and 2-6pm. Some shops are open longer, especially in tourist areas in the high season, when many of them are open 7 days a week. The banks are open 9am-12 noon and 2-4pm and are closed either Saturdays or Mondays. They close early the day before a bank holiday.

Post

As regards postal arrangements, it is possible to have items sent *poste restante* to head offices in the towns. The postcode for Corsica is F20, to which three figures are added for the individual local code — for example, 20 000 for Ajaccio, 20 200 for Bastia and 20 260 for Calvi.

The main post offices in the towns are open Mondays to Fridays 8am-7pm and Saturdays 8am-4pm. Small country post offices are closed 12 noon-2pm. Stamps are available at newsagents and tobacconists. The same applies to the *jetons* for use in public telephones, which can also be bought at restaurants and bars with a public telephone.

Public Holidays

The official holidays in France are as follows (apart from Sundays):

New Year	1 January
Easter Monday	(movable)
May Day	1 May
Ascension Day	(movable)
Whit Monday	(movable)
National Day	14 July
The Assumption	15 August
All Saints' Day	1 November
Armistice Day	
(1918)	11 November
Christmas Day	25 December

Armistice Day 1945 and the Feast of the Maid of Orléans (St Joan) are on 8 and 9 May respectively, but are officially celebrated on the second Sunday in May.

Tipping
Meal prices in restaurants and hotels include a 10 per cent to 15 per cent service charge. But it is normal to round the price up and include a tip depending on how good the service was. Porters are usually given a tip for carrying luggage (one franc per item). Usherettes in cinemas must also be tipped, one franc being the standard amount; tips are all the money they get, and sometimes they must actually pay for the privilege!

7. Language

Like the Corsicans themselves, the island dialects are in many ways a mixture. They are like all dialects of French and Italian in being based on dialects of Latin. But a large number of words have been borrowed from the other races that settled on the island. The Vandals and Goths left traces of ancient Germanic, while the Saracens left a considerable Arabic legacy. The Italians exerted by far the strongest and most lasting influence; but the most recent introductions have been from modern French and even English.

Although the island has only about 220,000 inhabitants, there are thought to be about eight distinct dialects of Corsican. The 'purest' of these is considered to be that spoken in Corte. The northern dialects are closer to the Tuscan dialects of Italy, while the dialects in the south are closer to those of northern Sardinia. The most distinctive feature of Corsican is the tendency to soften certain consonants between vowels. The name La Foce, for example, is pronounced as if it were La Voce (something like 'la voh-cheh').

A knowledge of Corsican is fortunately not necessary to make oneself understood! All Corsicans nowadays speak French, the island's official language — and most of them can understand Italian. Some English is spoken in resorts frequented by English-speaking tourists.

8. Useful French Words and Phrases

General Expressions

Hello — Bonjour
Good morning/afternoon — Bonjour
Good evening — Bonsoir
Good night — Bonne nuit
Goodbye — Au revoir
See you soon — A bientôt
yes/no — oui/non
please/thank you — s'il vous plaît/merci
Mr/Mrs/Miss — Monsieur/Madame/Mademoiselle
How are you? — Comment allez-vous?
Very well/unwell — Très bien/mal
I don't feel well — Je ne me sens pas bien
I'm very sorry — Tous mes regrets
I'm in a bad mood — Je suis de mauvaise humeur
What's new? — Quoi de neuf?
What's going on? — Que se passe-t-il?
Nothing — Rien
I have to go now — Je dois partir maintenant
I'm in a hurry — Je suis pressé
It's a shame — C'est dommage

Do you know Mr B? — Connaissez-vous Monsieur B?
May I introduce Mr B? — Puis-je vous présenter Monsieur B?
Pleased to meet you — Enchanté (de faire votre connaissance)
I'm an Englishman/Englishwoman/ — Je suis un(e) anglais(e)/
 American/American woman   un(e) américain(e)
Do you speak English? — Parlez-vous anglais?
I don't speak much French — Je ne parle pas beaucoup de
                                                          français
But I understand it — Mais je le comprends
I speak a little Italian — Je parle un peu d'italien
Yes, of course — Oui, naturellement
I said no — Je disais non
What were you saying? — Que disiez-vous?
Pardon? — Comment?
Excuse me, please — Excusez-moi, s'il vous plaît
Not at all — Il n'y a pas de quoi
Would you please... — Veuillez..., s'il vous plaît

That makes no difference to me — A moi, ça ne fais pas une
                                                      différence
I don't know — Je ne sais pas
Someone is knocking on the door — On frappe à la porte
Who is it? — Qui est là?
It's me — C'est moi
Come in — Entrez

The weather's nice — Il fait beau
It's very hot — Il fait très chaud
It's sunny — Il fait du soleil
The sun's just gone down — Le soleil vient de se coucher
It's getting dark — La nuit tombe
The moon is rising — La lune se lève
The weather's bad — Il fait mauvais temps
It's cold — Il fait froid
It's cloudy — Il est nuageux
It's raining — Il pleut
It's going to rain — Il va pleuvoir
There's thunder and lightning — Il tonne et éclaire
I can see a rainbow — Je vois un arc-en-ciel

What time is it? — Quelle heure est-il?
It's one o'clock — Il est une heure
It's quarter past two — Il est deux heures et quart
It's twenty past three — Il est trois heures vingt
It's half past four — Il est quatre heures et demi
It's quarter to five — Il est cinq heures moins le quart
It's ten to six — Il est six heures moins dix
At seven in the morning — A sept heures du matin
At eight in the evening — A huit heures du soir
It's not yet nine o'clock — Il n'est pas encore neuf heures
At three o'clock in the afternoon — A trois heures de l'après-midi

---

On Arrival

Miss A is arriving — Mademoiselle A arrive
Welcome! — Bienvenu!
Your passport, please — Votre passe-port, s'il vous plaît
How long do you wish to stay in — Combien de temps voulez-vous
  this country?   rester dans ce pays?
Only eighteen days — Seulement dix-huit jours

Sign here, please — Signez ici, s'il vous plaît
The customs — La douane
Have you anything to declare? — Avez-vous quelques choses à
                                                    déclarer?
No, I'm only carrying personal — Non, j'ai seulement des effets
   effects   personnels avec moi
First I need some money — D'abord j'ai besoin d'argent
Where can I change some currency? — Où est le bureau de
                                                    change?

Porter! — Porteur!
At your service — A votre service
Then I would like a taxi — Ensuite je voudrais un taxi
To Hotel X, please — A l'Hôtel X, s'il vous plaît
The address is... — L'adresse est...
Here we are — Voilà, nous sommes arrivés
Many thanks — Merci beaucoup
How much is it? — C'est combien?

At the Hotel

Have you any rooms free? — Avez-vous des chambres libres?
I would like... — Je voudrais bien...

a room with a bathroom	une chambre avec une salle de bain
a single room	une chambre pour une personne
a double room	une chambre pour deux personnes
a twin-bedded room	une chambre avec deux lits
a quiet room	une chambre tranquille

How much do you charge? — Quelles sont vos conditions?
Would you please give me the key — Pourriez-vous me donner
   to my room   la clef de ma chambre
I'm tired — Je suis fatigué
I don't want to be disturbed — Je ne veux pas être dérangé
Could you please wake me at six — Pourriez-vous me reveiller à
o'clock tomorrow morning   six heures demain
                                                    matin,s'il vous plaît
I would like to have breakfast in — J'aimerais le petit déjeuner
   my room   dans ma chambre
I shall be leaving at one o'clock — Je partirai demain à une heure
   tomorrow   le midi
Please ask the porter to bring my — Dites au porteur qu'il
   luggage down   descend mes bagages, s'il
                                                    vous plaît

Do you have a map of the — Avez-vous une carte touristique de
 area?   la ville et des environs?
I would like a trip round the town — Je voudrais faire un tour
                                              de ville
I would also like to see the area — Je voudrais aussi voir les
                                                environs
If anyone asks for me I'll be back — Si quelqu'un me demande je
 at seven o'clock   serai de retour à sept
                                              heures
Would you please call a taxi — Veuillez appeler un taxi

Where is the chambermaid? — Où est la femme de chambre?
Could you please wash and iron — Pourriez-vous laver et
 these things   repasser ces choses-là
Could you please have this cleaned — Pourriez-vous faire
                                                nettoyer cela
When will my things be ready? — Quand sont-ils prêts, les
                                              choses?
I've got a headache — J'ai mal de tête
I'm hot — J'ai chaud
I'm feeling ill — Je me sens malade
I need a doctor — J'ai besoin d'un médecin

At the Restaurant

I'm hungry — J'ai faim
I'm thirsty — J'ai soif
I'd like some breakfast — Je voudrais bien petit déjeuner
I'd like to eat — Je voudrais bien manger
Where is there a good, cheap — Où peut-on manger bien et pas
 restaurant?   trop cher
Is this table free? — Cette table, est-elle libre?
No, it's reserved — Non, elle est réservée
Waiter! — Garçon!
The menu, please — Le menu, s'il vous plaît
I'd like to try the local cuisine — Je voudrais essayer la cuisine du
                                                pays
Are the dishes highly spiced? — Est-ce que les plats sont
                                              épicés?
Is the wine included? — Le vin, est-il compris?
knife, fork, spoon — couteau, fourchette, cuiller
plate, cup, glass — assiette, tasse, verre

The bill, please — L'addition, s'il vous plaît
Where are the toilets? — Où se trouvent les toilettes?
gentlemen, men — messieurs, hommes
ladies, women — dames, femmes

---

breakfast — petit déjeuner
orange juice — jus d'orange
bread, rolls — pain, petits pains
butter — beurre
honey, jam — miel, confiture
marmalade — confiture d'oranges
ham, cheese — jambon, fromage
eggs and bacon — oeufs et lard
fried eggs — oeufs sur le plat
hard-boiled egg — oeuf dur
soft-boiled egg — oeuf à la coque
tea — thé
black coffee — café noir
white coffee — café au lait
coffee with cream — café crème
milk, sugar — lait, sucre
cocoa — chocolat

---

lunch, dinner, supper — déjeuner, diner, souper
clear soup — bouillon
I would like fish — Je voudrais du poisson
eel, trout, carp — anguille, truite, carpe
I would like meat — Je voudrais de la viande
boiled, grilled, roasted — cooked, grillé, rôti
rare, medium rare, well done — saignant, à point, bien cuit
beef — viande du boeuf
pork cutlet — côtelette du porc
fillet of veal — filet du veau
liver and kidneys — foie et rognons
tongue — langue
sausage — saucisse
turkey, chicken — dinde, poulet
goose, duck — oie, canard
pheasant, partridge — faisan, perdreau
wild boar — sanglier

---

salt, pepper, mustard — sel, poivre, moutarde

oil, vinegar — huile, vinaigre
vegetables — légumes
peas, lentils — petits pois, lentilles
(green) beans — haricots (verts)
cabbage, cauliflower — chou, chou-fleur
asparagus, artichokes — asperge, artichauts
carrots, beetroot — carottes, betteraves
onions, spinach — oignons, épinards
mushrooms — champignons
potatoes — pommes de terre
cucumber, lettuce — concombre, laitue

What would you like to drink? — Que désirez-vous à boire?
(iced) water — eau (glacée)
tomato juice — jus de tomate
light/brown ale — bière blonde/brune
red/white wine — vin rouge/blanc
dry/sweet wine — vin sec/doux
brandy — eau-de-vie
mineral water — eau minérale

---

ice — glace
cake, pastries — gâteau, pâtisseries
apples, pears, bananas — pommes, poires, bananes
pineapple, peaches — ananas, pêches
plums, apricots — prunes, abricots
strawberries, raspberries — fraises, framboises
grapes, cherries — raisins, cérises
lemons — citrons
citrons — cédrats

Shopping and Essentials

I have to do some shopping/errands — Je dois faire des courses
Where can one buy souvenirs? — Où peut-on acheter des
souvenirs?
It's a good shop — C'est un bon magasin
Please wait a moment — Veuillez attendre un petit moment
What would you like? — Que désirez-vous?
I'd like to buy a bag — Je voudrais acheter un sac
Show me some blouses — Montrez-moi des blouses
Have you anything else? — Avez-vous d'autres choses?

What does it cost? — Combien ça coûte?
Are your prices fixed? — Avez-vous des pris fixes?
It's very expensive — C'est très cher
Have you anything cheaper? — Avez-vous quelques choses de
                                                          meilleur marché?
Thank you, I'll be back — Merci, je serai de retour
Is there a photographic shop here? — Y a-t-il un magasin pour
                                                                photos?
I have a film to be developed and — J'ai une pellicule à
   printed   développer avec des
                                                     épreuves
black-and-white/colour — noir et blanc/de couleur
   transparency   diapositive

---

at the hairdresser's — chez le coiffeur
I'd like a shampoo and haircut, — S'il vous plaît lavez-moi la tête
   please   et coupez-moi les cheveux
I'd like a shampoo and set — Je voudrais bien une mise en plis
I'd like a shave, please — Faites-moi la barbe, s'il vous plaît

---

at the post office — au bureau de poste
Where is the *poste restante* — Où se trouve le guichet de poste
   counter?   restante?
Do you have any post for me? — Avez-vous des lettres pour moi?
How much does it cost to send a — Combien fait une lettre et une
   letter and a postcard   carte postale à
   to England (USA)?   déstination d'Angleterre?
                                               (d'Etats-Unis)
airmail — par avion
registered — recommandé
Do you have any special stamps? — Avez-vous des timbre
                                               spéciales?
Where is the postbox? — Où se trouve la boîte à lettres?

---

at the bank — à la banque
Where can I change a traveller's — A quel guichet peut-on
   cheque?   échanger un chèque de
                                               voyage?

---

at the pharmacist's — chez le pharmacien/dans la pharmacie
I'd like some pills for headache — Je voudrais des cachets contre
   and stomach-ache   le mal de tête et les maux
                                               d'estomac

I'd like something for diarrhoea — Je voudrais quelque chose
pour la diarrhée
I'd like some sticking plaster — Je voudrais de l'albuplast
Do you have any aspirin? — Avez-vous de l'aspirine?

In the Town

What is there to see in this town? — Quelles sont les curiosités
de cette ville?
Where is the market? — Où se trouve le marché?
I'd like to visit the cathedral — Je voudrais aller à la cathédrale
Is it far? — Est-il loin?
No, it's very close — Non, il est tout près
Follow this street — Suivez cette rue
At the end of the street — Au bout de la rue
At the next corner — Au coin prochain
Turn right/left — Tournez à droite/gauche
Go straight on — Allez tout droit
Cross the square — Traversez la place
Is the museum worth seeing? — Ça vaut la peine de voir le
musée?
Excuse me, is this the way to the — Excusez-moi, est-ce que
station? c'est le chemin pour la
gare?
Where does this street go? — Où nous conduit cette rue?
How do I find the theatre? — Comment va-t-on au théâtre?
You can go on foot — On peut aller à pied
Where are you going? — Où allez-vous?
What bus should I take? — Quel autobus dois-je prendre?
Where does the bus go from? — Où départ l'autobus?
The bus stop is opposite the bank — L'arrêt se trouve en face de
la banque
Where is the taxi rank? — Où est la station de taxis?
Could you please drive me into the — Conduisez-moi s'il vous
town centre plaît dans le centre
Stop here — Arrêtez-vous ici
Wait for me here — Attendez-moi ici
Wait a few minutes — Attendez quelques minutes
Excuse me, can you tell me...? — Excusez-moi, pouvez-vous me
dire...?
Are we allowed to take photographs? — Peut-on photographier
ici?

Only with special permission — Seulement avec permission
entrance, exit — entrée, sortie
open, closed — ouvert, fermé
pull, push — tirez, poussez
Entry free — Entrée libre
No way through — Pas de passage à travers
No entry — Accès interdit
No smoking — Ne pas fumer

Travelling

at the travel agent's — au bureau de voyage
I'd like a trip to Calvi — Je voudrais faire un tour à Calvi
How do you want to travel? — Par quel moyen voulez-vous partir?
The train only goes once a day — Le train part seulement une fois
par jour
Give me a single — Donnez-moi un billet aller
A return, please — Un retour, s'il vous plaît
Reserve a seat for me too — Faites-moi aussi une réservation
I'd like a seat by the window in a — Je voudrais une place auprès
smoking compartment   de la fenêtre dans un
fumeur
Do you have any brochures and — Avez-vous des itinéraires et
itineraries?   des prospectus?
Many thanks for the information — Merci beaucoup pour le
renseignement

I'd like to hire a car — Je voudrais louer une auto
Are the roads good? — Les routes, sont-elles bonnes?
The road is very twisty — La route fait beaucoup de virages
It's up in the mountains — C'est dans les montagnes
How far is it from here to Bastia? — Ça fait combien de kilomètres
d'ici à Bastia?

Which is...   Quel est...
the nicest way?   le plus beau chemin?
the quickest way?   le chemin le plus rapide?
the shortest way?   le chemin le plus court?
I need some petrol (gasolene)— J'ai besoin d'essence
I'll have twenty litres of petrol (gasolene)— Je prends vingt litres
and some oil for the engine   d'essence et de
l'huile pour le moteur
Twenty litres of four-star, please — Vingt litres de super, s'il vous
plaît

Could you wipe the windscreen and — Pouvez-vous nettoyer le
   check the tyre pressures?   parebrise et vérifier la
                                           pression des pneus?

I've broken down — Je suis en panne

Could you tow me to a garage? — Pouvez-vous me remorquer
                                      jusqu'au garage?

The battery is flat — La batterie est vide

The carburettor needs cleaning and — On doit nettoyer le
   the spark-plugs need changing   carburateur et changer
                                     les bougies

The brakes are working badly — Les freins ne fonctionnent pas
                                    bien

Take care! — Attention!

Good luck! — Bonne chance!

FURTHER INFORMATION

The information given in this chapter is for general guidance only as it is subject to change. Continually updated information is available from banks, travel agents, the French Government Tourist Office and Consulates.

Museums, Monuments and Places of Interest

Admission charges have not been included as they are subject to change. Opening times also vary so it is advisable to check with the local tourist information office before setting out. Addresses and telephone numbers have been included where possible.

Archaeological Museum
Albertacce
☎ 95480105 (Town Hall)
History and prehistory of Nioli.

Archaeological Museum
Levie
☎ 95784437
Open: June-September,10am-12 noon, 3-7pm; October-May, 2-4pm.

Archaeological Museum of Prehistoric Corsica
Rue Croce
20100 Sartène

☎ 95770109/95771540
Open: 15 June-15 September, 10am-12 noon, 2-6pm; 16 September-14 June, 10am-12 noon, 2-5pm.

Capitelle Museum
18 Boulevard Danielle-Casanova
Ajaccio
☎ 95215057
Ajaccio of the eighteenth and nineteenth centuries.
Open: daily, 9am-12 noon, 3-7pm, closed Sunday 12 noon-Monday 3pm.

Cervione Museum
Cervione
☎ 95381283
History, archaeology, ethnology, religious art.

Chapelle Impériale
Rue Fesch
Ajaccio
☎ 95215057
Built 1857 under Napoléon III
Open: daily except Sunday, 9-11am, 2-5pm.

Chapelle of St-Antoine
Citadelle
Calvi
Religious objects.
Open: daily except Sunday 10am-12noon, 3-6pm.

Fesch Museum
Rue Fesch
Ajaccio
☎ 95214817
Collection of 1,200 paintings.
France's most important collection
of Italian masterpieces apart from
the Louvre. Also library containing
40,000 volumes.

Filitosa Museum
(20km from Propriano)
☎ 95510094
Stones and statues from 6000-
3000 years ago. Most famous site
on Corsica.
Open: daily, 8am-8pm.

**Jérôme Carcopino
Archaeological Museum**
Fort Matra
20270 Aléria
☎ 95570092
Archaeological finds.
Open: daily except Sunday,
8am-12 noon, 2-6.30pm; 2-5pm
only in winter.

Maison Bonaparte
Rue St-Charles
Ajaccio
☎ 95214389
Built beginning of eighteenth
century — Napoléon born here.
Open: daily, 10am-12 noon, 2-5pm,
except Sunday until Monday 2pm.

Monte Bughju
Maccinaggio
☎ 95354257
Archaeological dig of Roman site.

**Museum of Corsican
Ethnography**
Palais des Gouvernement
Citadelle
Place du Donjon-de-la-Citadelle

Bastia
☎ 95310912/95321699
Ethnography, costumes, customs,
lifestyles and religion.
Open: daily, 9am-12 noon, 3-6pm.
Free entrance Wednesdays.

Napoléon Museum
Town Hall
Place Maréchal Foch
Ajaccio
☎ 95219015
Paintings, documents of Imperial
Age.
Open: daily except Sunday, 9am-
12 noon, 2-5pm.

Pasquale Paoli's House
Morosaglia
☎ 95476003
Objects, souvenirs, birthplace of
Paoli.

Seneca Museum
Luri
☎ 95350015 (Town Hall)
Medieval ceramics.

**Other Places of Interest,
Well Worth Visiting May be
Found at:**

Ajaccio
Palais Fesch: houses treasures
bequeathed by Napoléon's uncle,
Cardinal Fesch.
Milleli: north-west of Ajaccio,
Bonaparte summer residence.

Algajola
Massive seventeenth-century
fortress.

Bastia
Citadel: massive edifice.
Fort Lacroix and Fort Strafello: two
interesting old Forts.

Governor's Palace: fourteenth-
century museum on ground floor.
Palais de Justice: interesting
architecture, blue marble columns.

Bonifacio
St Anthony's Grotto: east of
Bonifacio, stalactites.
Grotte du Sdragonato: boat trip
west of Bonifacio; roof of cave has
hole the shape of Corsica.

Calvi
Citadel: ramparts date to 1545.
Governor's Palace: eighteenth
century, houses foreign legion
parachute regiment.
Palais Giubega: fifteenth-century
Bishop's palace, belonged to
Napoléon's godfather Laurent
Giubega.
Tour du Cel: massive round tower
used for storing salt, fifteenth
century.

Castello
Castello Castle: ruins, belonged to
Gentile family.

Cauria
Megalithic sites: two double rows of
menhirs (alignments).

Ceccia
Tower temple: built 1323 BC.

Col de Serra
Moulin Mattei: near Ersa, windmill
converted into the Mattei firm
advertisement for its wine and
cédratine liqueur; hostelry.

Corbara
Corbara Abbey: built 1431 as
orphanage, turned into Franciscan
monastery.

Corte
Palais National: contains
interesting museum of history and
prehistory of Corsica. Was the seat
of government of Pasquale Paoli.

Favellelo
Paladin: a menhir, 2.9m high, 1½
tonnes.

Furiani
Genoese fortress remains,
captured by Corsicans 1729.

Girolata
Girolata ruins: ruins of Genoese
fort.

Mariana (Roman settlement)
St Mary's Basilica (La Canonica):
built twelfth century.

Olmeto
Castello della Rocca: ruins of
thirteenth-century castle belonging
to della Rocca family, Corsican
nobles.

Piana
Foce d'Orto: ruined fort near Piana.
Les Calanches: Corsica's most
amazing natural phenomenon —
bizarre cliffs, 12km beyond Piana.

Pigna
Handicrafts collection: near Pigna
church.

Poggio
Tour de Sénèque: Genoese tower
where Seneca was said to have
lived.

Pozzo-di-Borgo
Château de la Punta: Louis Quinze
style.

Ponte Nuovo
Genoese bridge.
Monument: pyramid-shaped, commemorating battle of Ponte Nuovo.

St Florent
Citadel: ruined fifteenth-century fortifications.
Ste Marie de Nebbio: fascinating thirteenth-century basilica, Pisan-style in marble.

Tiuccia
Ruined castle of the Count of Cinarca.

Tizzano Valley
Alignement i Stantura, Alignements de Palaggiu (90 double rows of menhirs), Alignement de Renaggiu and the Dolmen of Fontenacciu—the finest and the best on Corsica.
Frate e Sora: two menhirs dating back to 2000 BC.

Torre
Bronze Age tower: prehistoric remains.

Churches and Cathedrals

Ajaccio
Cathedral: contains white marble font in which Napoléon was baptised, built 1554-93.
Chapelle des Grecs: built for Greeks who fled Paomina.
Chapelle Impériale: housed in Palais Fesch, several members of Bonaparte family buried here.
Church of St Roch: built in 1895.
St Erasmus' Church: dedicated to seafarers in 1815.
St John the Baptist: fourteenth-century church.

Aléria
St Mark's church: built 1462.

Alesani
Monastery with fine statues.

Algajola
Church with impressive paintings.

Aregno
Fourteenth-century church built out of pale limestone and blue slate, fifteenth-century frescos.

Asco
Seventeenth-century church of St Michel.

Bastelica
Interesting fourteenth-century church.

Bastia
Cathedral of St John the Baptist: founded 1640, Baroque façade added in eighteenth century, with Corsican marble altar.
Chapelle de l'Immaculée Conception: 1950, genuine murillo altarpiece.
Chapelle de St Roch: 1604 with statue of St Roch in multicoloured marble.
Chapelle Ste-Croix: eighteenth-century gold stucco decorations. Built to house black wooden crucifix, the Christ of Miracles.
St Mary's church: founded 1495, served as cathedral for diocese of Mariana at one time. Fifteenth-century painting of the Assumption.

Bicchisano
Interesting white church.

Bonifacio
Chapelle St Roch: a seamen's church.
St Dominic's: octagonal bell tower and cluster of small spires: Corsica's only substantial Gothic church.
St Erasmus church: small church on the harbourfront.
Ste Marie-Majeur: important church with triple naved structure, Pisan and Genoese Gothic features, third-century pre-Christian, sarcophagus.

Calacuccia
St Peter's Church: carved wooden statue of Christ.

Calenzana
Church of St Blaise (La Collegiata): built 1700, multicoloured marble, Baroque decorations.
Sta Restituta: mix of architectural styles, parts date back to fifteenth century.

Calvi
St Andrew's Oratory: only example of Renaissance church on Corsica.
St John the Baptist cathedral: sixteenth-century multicoloured marble altar.
St Mary of the Assumption: eighteenth-century church with dome topped by Baroque lantern.

Carbini
Fourteenth-century Romanesque church of St Jean with decorated arch.

Cargèse
Greek Orthodox church: icons of saints.

Carcheto
Church contains beautifully simple representation of the stations of the cross.

Castello
Notre Dame des Neiges: built thirteenth century, fourteenth-century frescos.

Cervione
St Christine's church: twin apse — Pisan feature only found on Corsica.
St Mary and St Erasmus: sixteenth-century domed cathedral

Corbara
Lovely Baroque church.

Corte
Church of the Annunciation: seventeenth-century, Baroque bell tower, wooden tabernacles, beautiful pulpit.

Gulf of Sta Manza
St Julien: twelfth to thirteenth-century convent with Gothic features.

Lavasina
Interesting seventeenth-century church with Madonna painting with supposedly miraculous properties.

Levie
Church with medieval ivory statue of Christ.

Lumio
Interesting church with modern façade, old Baroque bell tower.

Macinaggio
Sta Maria della Chiapella: restored in eighteenth century, twin apse.

Mariana
La Canonica (Basilica of St Mary):
founded 1120, destroyed sixteenth-
century, rebuilt and reconsecrated.
San Parteo: Romanesque church
with white marble columns.

Montemaggiore
St Rainier: thirteenth-century dark
and light stone chapel.

Murato
St Michael's: rectangular church of
blue and white mosaic stone with
unique bell tower.

Nonza
Sta Julia's: sixteenth century
church, marble altar with
centrepiece.

Oletta
Church with sixteenth-century
triptych and miraculous picture of
Madonna.

Omessa
Baroque church tower.
Château de Bellevue monastery.

Piana
St Mary's church — beautiful bell
tower.

Pigna
Unusual church, domes on both
towers above façade, probably of
Moorish influence.

Piazelli
St François d'Alesani: abbey where
Corsican constitution was drafted,
beautiful sculptures.

Piedicroce
Baroque church of St Peter and
St Paul.

Porto-Vecchio
Church of Ste Croix: the most
interesting building in the town,
nineteenth-century paintings.

Quenza
St Mary: Romanesque chapel
dated AD1000; oldest surviving
church on Corsica.

Rapale
Romanesque chapel of San
Cesareo.

Sagone
Remains of old twelfth-century
cathedral, built around the apse of
a fourth-century church.

San Nicolao
Baroque church with separate bell
tower.

San Pietro-di-Tenda
Church of reddish stone with
separate bell tower.

Sisco
St Michael's: Romanesque with
frieze.
St Martin's: copper mask, hand-
forged gold and silver designs.

Soccia
Church with beautiful fifteenth-
century triptych.

Soria
Sta Marguerita: Romanesque
chapel.

Ste Marie-Siché
Old church at entrance to village
with lattice-work tower.

St Florent
Ste Marie de Nebbio: Pisan church.

Vico
St Francis' Monastery: built late
fifteenth-century by Corsican
freedom fighter. Contains remains
of old wooden crucifix the first
monks brought over from Italy.

Annual Events

Good Friday
Sartène
The Catenacciu — a procession.

3 May
Bastia
Annual procession.

18th May
Lavasina near Bastia
Festival of the Mother of God —
Corsican equivalent of Lourdes.

2 June
Ajaccio
St Erasmus' Day — special
procession.

15 August
Bastia
Festival of the Assumption.

Sunday after 8 September
Calvi
Festival of the Madonna, Madonna
della serra church.

8-10 September
Casamaccioli
Feast of the Nativity of the Virgin —
folk festival and religious event.

For further information about fêtes
and festivals, contact the
Syndicats d'Initiative, and *Offices
de Tourism.*

Travelling to Corsica

By Air
See page 182. Pan Am run direct
flights from New York, to Nice and
to Rome from where connections
may be caught to Corsica. Air
France runs flights to Corsica from
Birmingham, London and
Manchester airports.

Air Inter is France's national
domestic airline, flying between
Paris and thirty cities and towns
including airports on Corsica. Air
France and Air Inter provide daily
connections throughout the year
and this includes the airline TAT
during the summer season. As a
guideline, here are some average
fares (single ticket to Corsica,
1987 prices) and average flight
times:

950F from Paris (1 hr 30 min)
351F from Marseille (40 min)
300F from Nice (30 min)

Many companies offer various
discounts and special fares for
children, newly-weds, regular
users, young people, foreigners
and elderly people. For more
information contact the airlines
themselves.

By Rail
French railways (SNCF) operate a
nationwide network serving over
6000 destinations. Motorail
services carry cars and
passengers overnight on the same
train from various destinations.
Under 26s qualify for a 50 per cent
reduction on rail travel with a Carré
jeune or Carte jeune. This card can
be obtained from French Railways
or French railway stations.

By Sea

For information regarding ferry links from Great Britain to France contact the French Government Tourist Office or the shipping companies themselves. SNCM (Société Maritime Corse Méditerranée) provides services linking France and Corsica every day during the season and twice a week during winter. Ships leave Marseille, Nice and Toulon for Ajaccio, Bastia, Calvi, Ile Rousse and Propriano. Crossing varies between 5 and 10 hours depending on the route. Discounts are the same as those offered by the French railways. There are three periods of fares: the 'white' period during season; the 'blue' period, off season (fares equivalent to 50 per cent of the 'white' period) (motorvehicles and passengers); 'red' period in the high season (July to August).

There are also regular car-ferry links with Italy from Genoa (7 hours) and Livorno (4 hours) to Bastia and return.

Travelling on Corsica

By Air

Corse Aéro Service and Air Corse provide flights within Corsica and abroad.
Corse Aéro Service —
(Ajaccio) ☎ 95232142
Corse Aéro ☎ Service —
(Propriano) ☎ 95760499
Air Corse —
(Ajaccio Airport) ☎ 95206130

By Coach

See page 186.

Coaches or buses depart regularly from Ajaccio to a variety of destinations including Bastia, Calvi, Porto-Vecchio, Bonifacio, Evisa, Tiuccia, Sagone, Vico and Propriano. Buses/coaches depart regularly from Bastia and travel to Ajaccio, Corte, Porto-Vecchio, Ile Rousse and Calvi: For further information contact the coach stations, *Syndicats d'Initiative* and *Offices de Tourisme*.

Hire Cars
Mopeds/Bicycles

See page 185. See also Useful Addresses.

By Rail

See page 185. Corsican railways covers some 230km, running through Ajaccio, Corte, Bastia, Ile Rousse, Calvi etc; in fact all the main towns. There is a daily service between Ajaccio and Bastia and back (3 hours).
Here are some 1987 fares:

Ajaccio — Calvi	95F
Ajaccio — Corte	44F
Bastia — Corte	39F
Ajaccio — Bastia	82F
Bastia — Calvi	62F

Motoring in Corsica

See page 185.

CBs

Equipment operating on 26,960-27,410Mhz may be imported and used by short-term visitors holding a licence. Power must not exceed 4 watts, however, and the maximum number of channels is 40.

Drink/Driving

Drivers found to have a blood alcohol level of 0.8gms/1000 or over or whose breath is found to contain 0.4mgs/litre could receive a 1 month to1 year prison sentence and/or fine of 800-8000F and could have their licences withdrawn.

Insurance

Fully comprehensive cover is advisable. Although a green card is no longer compulsory it will provide excellent cover. Contact your insurance company before departing. Some motoring organisations like the British AA or the American AAA may have special insurance schemes for members.

Lights

Beams are to be adjusted for right-hand driving if you are used to driving on the left. Yellow tinted headlights are not compulsory but advisable. Car drivers must use dipped or parking lights at all times, motorcyclists must use dipped headlights at all times except when stationary.

Hooting

No hooting between dusk and sunrise — flashing headlights are to be used instead. Hooting is prohibited in built-up areas except where there is immediate danger.

Motorcycles/Mopeds

Up to 50cc — must not exceed 45km/h. Minimum age 14, no licence required, forbidden on motorways.

51cc-80cc — maximum speed 75km/h, minimum age 16, full licence required.

81cc-400cc — maximum speed as for cars, minimum age 18, full licence required.

Over 400cc — as above but heavy motorcycle licence required. Crash helmets must be worn, national identity plates must be attached and adequate insurance cover taken out. Motorcyclists must use dipped headlights at all times except when stationary.

Parking

Inside a built-up area stationary or parked vehicles must be placed on the right-hand side on dual carriageways and on either side on single carriageways unless specified. Outside built-up areas vehicles must be parked as far away from the roadway as possible.

In large towns, cars may not be parked for longer than 24 hours in any one place and in certain streets on one side of the street only — look out for signs.

Requirements

You need to display a national identity plate on your vehicle near to the national registration plate. You must carry with you the original of the vehicle's registration document, full national driving licence and current insurance certificate plus a note of authorisation from the owner if the vehicle is not registered in your name.

Rules of the Road

On Corsica you drive on the right. In built-up areas, the *priorité* rule still applies and you must give way to anybody coming out of a side-turning on the right. On traffic islands or roundabouts give way to cars already on the roundabout.

Speed Limits
In built-up areas — 60km/h unless specified. Outside built-up areas — 90km/h, in rain and snow etc, 80km/h. On bypass motorways and dual carriageways — 110km/h, in rain and snow etc, 100km/h. On trunk motorways — 130km/h, in rain, snow etc, 110km/h.
The minimum fine for speeding is 1300F.

Vehicle Size
Drivers of vehicles with a height of 13ft including load must keep a constant watch to see no damage is done to overhead structures or vegetation. Maximum width — 8ft 2½ in; maximum length — vehicle, 36ft, trailers,36ft.

Vital Points
Minimum driving age in France is 18.
No driving on a provisional licence. Seat belts must be worn by driver and front-seat passenger. No children under 10 are allowed in the front of a vehicle. Carry a complete spare bulb kit and use a left-hand external mirror. Red warning triangles are to be carried unless your vehicle has hazard warning lights.

Winter Driving
If necessary snow chains may be bought from hypermarkets in mountain areas. Studded tyres may be used from 15 November to 15 March on vehicles weighing less than 3500kg but the speed limit is 90km/h and a disc reading '90' must be fixed to the vehicle.

Accommodation

Camping
See p 188. Sites fall into 1 to 4-star grades. A 1-star site might charge (1987 prices) 55F per day for a family of four with car. Visitors to Corsica will find a wide variety of campsites. Except for registered sites, permission must be sought from the land owner. Camping is forbidden along the sea shore. A guide to registered camping/caravan sites is available from L'Agence Régionale du Tourisme et des Loisirs — see Useful Addresses.

Holiday Villages
There are about fifty holiday villages on Corsica offering various stays at inclusive prices including meals or self-catering facilities and leisure, sporting and cultural activities. Some are naturist villages only. Again, a guide is published by L'Agence Régionale du Tourisme et des Loisirs.

Hotels
See page 186. A complete list of hotels is available from the French Government Tourist Office.
 The majority of Corsica's hotels are newly-built, of good quality and are mainly situated on the coast. It is advisable to book in advance
 Hotels in France fall into five categories: 1-star to Luxury 4-star. An average comfortable 2-star hotel might charge (1987 prices) from 110-220F for a room for two people. Breakfast is usually extra and might cost about 15-20F per person (1987). Many chains offer a free bed for a child under 12

sleeping in the parents' room. Most hotels having their own restaurant expect visitors to take dinner if spending the night. Room plus all meals (full board or *pension*) are usually offered for a stay of 3 days or longer. Half-board (*demi-pension* — room, breakfast, one meal) terms are usually available outside peak holiday period and some in season.

'Rural' Holidays

Chambres d'Hôte are fully-fitted rooms in farmhouses and provide bed and breakfast. A '*Gîte rural*' is a fully-furnished house graded according to the degree of comfort. A guide to this kind of accommodation may be obtained from the Comité Régional des Gîtes Ruraux et L'Agence Régionale du Tourisme et des Loisirs — see Useful Addresses.

Tips for Travellers

Banks

May be found at Aléria, Bastia, Ajaccio, Borgo, Bonifacio, Ghisonaccia, Ile Rousse, Cargèse, Calvi, Corte, Moriani, Pietranera, Porto-Vecchio, Porto, Propriano, Sagone, Vico, St Florent and Sartène, but for a more comprehensive list obtain a copy of 'Corsica — the holiday island' from the French Government Tourist Office.

Business Hours
See page 194.

Credit Cards
Visa, Mastercard/Access, Diners'

Club, and Eurocard are accepted in many hotels, restaurants, shops and filling stations. They are not usually accepted in hypermarkets.

Currency and Exchange
Unlimited currency may be taken into France but must be declared if bank notes to the value of 12,000F or more are likely to be re-exported. On entering France, if you have more than the equivalent of 12,000F in foreign notes you are advised to complete a *Déclaration d'entrée en France de billets de banque étrangers*. You are required to submit the form on leaving France if you are re-exporting more than 12,000F.

Exchange rate at February 1987:
£1 = 9.8F
$1 = 6.1 F

French currency comprises
500, 200, 100, 50, 20 and 10F notes; 10, 5, 2, 1 and ½F coins; 20, 10 and 5 centime coins.

Customs
See page 183.

Disabled
Send a stamped addressed envelope for a special information sheet to the French Government Tourist Office.

Electricity
220V, 2 pin plugs or occasionally 3-pin round plugs are used. Take an adaptor.

Food and Drink
See page 188. Wines and Corsican regional specialities may be

obtained from: Etablissement Ecopral, 42 Rue de l'Ourcq, 75019 Paris ☎ (1) 42392300; Union of Wine Producers of the Island of Beauty, 138 Rue Sadi-Carnot, 93170 Bagnolet, ☎ (1) 43611630 and, of course, the island itself.

Medical Advice
See page 183. British citizens should check with the DHSS to see if they are eligible for emergency cover under form E111. US citizens should contact their insurance carrier to discover coverage, claims procedure and reimburse-ment. Vaccinations are not normally required but check before departing.

Newspapers
Corse Matin (daily); *La Corse* (daily); *Kyrn* (monthly)

Passports/Visas
See page 183.

Post
See page 194. Letters can be sent for collection c/o Poste Restante, Poste Centrale in the town visited. The fee is small and proof of identification is needed.

Radio
France Inter, the French radio station broadcasts on 1829m longwave. Radio Corse International, 20200 Bastia, Tel: 95321695 broadcasts daily:
Longwave FM
  Ajaccio — 100.5 MHz
  Bastia — 101.7MHz
  Calvi — 92.6MHz
  Corte — 100MHz
  Ile Rousse — 88.3MHz
  Porto-Vecchio — 101.8MHz

Tax-Free Shopping
Any person over 15 staying in France for less than 6 months but who is normally resident abroad is entitled to have VAT deducted from purchases.

The following may not be purchased tax-free: food products, tobacco, medicines, weapons, (other than the smooth bore sporting guns), gold and loose precious stones, collectors' works of art and antiques worth more than 10,000F, spare parts and accessories for private transport, goods for resale.

For residents of the EEC the value of purchases (including tax) must not be less than 2400F per item or set of items; for non-EEC residents the value must not be less than 1200F.

When a purchase is made, a passport or other proof of residence outside France must be shown. The vendor will provide you with an export sales invoice (*bordereau*) at the time of purchase. You should complete and sign this and have it stamped by the customs as follows:
For residents in the EEC (yellow form)
When you return home:
• Have three sheets (two yellow and one green) stamped by the Customs and Excise office of your country of residence outside France.
• You should yourself then return the two yellow sheets to the Bureau des Douanes de Paris-Le Chapelle, 61, Rue de la Chapelle, 75018 Paris.
• Keep the green sheet.
For residents outside the EEC (pink form)

When you leave France:
• Show your goods and the invoice to the French Customs at the point of exit (3) with the stamped envelope given to you by the vendor.
• The French Customs take the pink sheets and stamp and return to you the green sheet which you should keep in the event of any dispute.
• After checking, the French Customs forwards the yellow or pink sheets to the vendor, who then refunds to you the amount shown on the invoice, unless he did so at the time of purchase. This does not dispense you from the Customs formalities.

Telephones

Use a public coin box or telephone counter at a Post Office. If a café, hotel or restaurant is used, it is likely that the call will cost up to 30 per cent more! If you have a *Telecard* you do not need change and a booth equipped with a card-operated payphone can be used. *Telecards* may be purchased from Post Offices, railway ticket offices or shops displaying the 'Telecarte' sign.

   Reduced rates apply Monday to Friday, 9.30pm-8am and Saturdays from 2pm for the Common Market, Switzerland and Spain and 10pm-9am for Canada and the USA.

   Reduced rates apply for the above countries on Sundays and on French Bank Holidays.

How to Use Pay Phones

Use a 1F coin for untimed calls. Other coins accepted are ½F and 5F. Insert a coin (coins are taken smallest first).

Wait for dial tone (steady tone).
Dial number.
When finished, hang up and unused coins are returned.

Useful Numbers

Information, directory enquiries: 12
Long distance operator: 10
Operator: 13
Fire: 18
Police: 17
Ambulance: 18
24-hour English SOS line (Paris):
☎ 7238080

Dialling Codes

UK to France: 010 33
France to UK: 19 44
US to France: 011 33
France to US: 19 1
When dialling from France to the UK, the zero prefixed to the STD code should be omitted.

Temperature Guide

Average air temp. ˚C

J	F	M	A
13	12	14	16
M	**J**	**J**	**A**
21	25	28	28
S	**O**	**N**	**D**
26	21	18	14

Average air temp. ˚F

J	F	M	A
55	53	57	61
M	**J**	**J**	**A**
70	77	82	82
S	**O**	**N**	**D**
79	70	64	57

Time

For most of the year Corsica is one hour ahead of Greenwich Mean Time, i.e. it is under Central European Time.

Water

Water served in hotels and restaurants is usually safe. Do not drink from taps labelled *eau non potable* — not drinking water.

Local Tourist Information

Once in Corsica, contact the local *Offices de Tourisme* or *Syndicats d'Initiative* for local information.

Ajaccio
Hôtel de ville
Place Foch
20000 Ajaccio
☎ 95215339/95214087

Aléria
Mairie
20270 Aléria
☎ 95570073

Asco and Haut-Asco
Mairie d'Asco
Asco
☎ 95478207

Bastia
35 Boulevard Paoli
Place St-Nicholas
20200 Bastia
☎ 95310089

Bonifacio
Rue Longue BP35
20169 Bonifacio
☎ 95730348

Calvi
Chemin de la Plage
20260 Calvi
☎ 95650587

Cargèse
Rue du Dr Dragacci
20130 Cargèse
☎ 95264131

Corte
La Citadelle
20250 Corte
☎ 95460159

Ghisonaccia
Mairie
20240 Ghisonaccia
☎ 95561510

Ile Rousse
Place Paoli
20220 Ile Rousse
☎ 95600435

Porticcio
20166 Porticcio
☎ 95250574

Porto
On Route de la Marine
20150 Porto
☎ 95261055

Porto-Vecchio
Place de l'Hôtel de Ville
20137 Porto-Vecchio
☎ 95700958

Propriano
17 Cours du Gal-de-Gaulle
20110 Propriano
☎ 95760149

Quenza
Mairie
Quenza
☎ 95786211

St Florent
Immeuble Ste Anne
20217 St Florent
☎ 95370604

Sartène
Rue Borgo
20100 Sartène
☎ 95771540

Solenzara
Mairie Annexe
20223 Solenzara
☎ 95574151

Tiuccia Cinarca
Cinarca Hotel
20111 Tiuccia
☎ 95522139

Zivaco
Mairie
Zivaco
☎ 95244005

Useful Addresses

Accommodation

American Youth Hostel Association
1332 'I' Street N.W
Suite 800
Washington DC 20005
☎ (202) 7836161

Chambres Départmentales de
 l'Hôtellerie et du Tourisme
Hôtel Albion
20000 Ajaccio
(Corse-du-Sud)

Chambres Départmentales de
 l'Hôtellerie et du Tourisme
Hôtel Isola
20190 Borg.

Comité de Liaison du Tourisme
 (Social et Associatif)
24 Boulevard Paoli
20200 Bastia
☎ 95227079

Fédération Française de Camping/
 Caravanning
(Délégué Régional de Haute -
 Corse)
M. Pascal Molinetti
Corse Hygiène
11 Rue Luce de Casabianca
20200 Bastia
(Délégué Départemental Corse-du-
 Sud)
M. Jean Maiboroda
Villa Mariaccia
Route du Salario
20000 Ajaccio

Fédération Régionale de l'Hôtellerie
 du Plein Air Camping
20166 Porticcio
☎ 95200051

G.I.E. Loisirs Accueil Région Corse
24 Boulevard Paoli
20000 Ajaccio
☎ 95227079

Relais Régional des Gîtes Ruraux
22 Boulevard Paoli
20177 Ajaccio
☎ 95221460

YHA (ENG)
14 Southampton Street
London WC2E 7HE
☎ (01) 8368541

Advice and Information

Consulates

American Consulate
9 Rue Armeny
13006 Marseille
☎ (91) 549200

American Consulate
1 Rue du Maréchal Joffre
06000 Nice
☎ (91) 888955/888772

American Embassy
2 Av Gabriel
75382 Paris
☎ (1) 2961202

British Embassy
35 Rue du Fauborg St-Honore
F-75008 Paris
☎ (1) 42669142
(British embassies also at Nice and
Marseille)

French Consulate General
Visa Department
College House
Wright's Lane
London W8
☎ (01) 9371202

French Consulate General
(including Custom's enquiries)
24 Rutland Gate
London SW7 1DH
☎ (01) 5815292

French Consulate
934 Fifth Avenue
New York
NY 10021
☎ (212) 5350100

French Embassy
58 Knightsbridge
London SW1X 7JT
☎ (01) 2358080

Crafts

9 Rue Notre-Dame, Ajaccio
5 Rue des Terrasses, Bastia
13 Rue Colonel Ferracci, Corte
Chemin de Paomina, Cargèse

Sport

Canoeing
M. Santonacci
Route des Sanguinaires
20000 Ajaccio
☎ 95213946

Clay Pigeon Shooting
Association Ajacienne du
  Tir au Vol
Stand Municipal de Parata
Route des Sanguinaires
☎ 95222705

Fishing
Fédération Départementale de
Pêche
  et de Pisciculture
7 Boulevard Paoli
Bastia
☎ 95314731

Flying/Parachuting
Aéroclub d'Ajaccio
Airport Campo dell'Oro
20000 Ajaccio
☎ 95211857

Aéroclub de Bastia
Airport Bastia-Poretta
20200 Bastia
☎ 95362485

Hunting and Shooting
Fédération Départementale des
  Chasseurs de la Corse-du-Sud
19 Av Bévérini
20000 Ajaccio
☎ 95231691

Fédération Départementale des
  Chasseurs de Haute-Corse
Résidence Nouvelle-Corniche
St Joseph
20200 Bastia
☎ 95322599

Potholing
Association Spéléologique Corse
2 Rue Martinetti
20000 Ajaccio
☎ 95216821

Riding
Association Régionale pour le
 Tourisme Equestre
9 Boulevard Pugliesi-Conti
20000 Ajaccio
☎ 95214879

Scuba Diving
Fédération Française d'Etudes
 et de Sports Sous-marins
25 Boulevard Dominique-Paoli
20000 Ajaccio
☎ 95222378

Tennis
Tennis Club de Mezzavia
Col Stiletto
Ajaccio
☎ 95201408

Walking Tours/Hiking
Association 'I Muntagnoli Corsi'
Quartier Sta-Maria
20122 Quenza
☎ 95746229/95782125

Muntagne Corse in Liberta
Parc Bilello
Immeuble Girolata
Av Napoléon III
20000 Ajaccio
☎ 95231742/95227079

Parc Régional
Palais Lantivy
20000 Ajaccio
☎ 95215654

Watersports
Obtain the brochure 'Corse
Nautique, from the French
Government Tourist Office or
contact L'Agence Régionale du
Tourisme et des Loisirs.

Travel

Air France
3 Boulevard du Roi Jérôme
Ajaccio
☎ 95210061

Air France
6 Av Emile Sari
Bastia
☎ 95312774/95319931

Air France (UK)
158 New Bond Street
London W1Y 0AY
☎ (01) 4999511/(01) 4998611

Air France (US)
666 Fifth Avenue
New York, NY10019
☎ (212) 8417301

Air France
7 Av Gustave V
Nice
☎ 93213232

Air France
119 Champs-Elysées
Paris
☎ (1)42992364

Air Inter
Ajaccio
☎ 95216306

Air Inter
Bastia Airport
☎ 95360295

Air Inter
Rue du Père-Corentin
Paris
☎ (1)45392525

British Airways
London Air Terminal
Cromwell Road
London SW7 4ED
☎ (01) 8974000

British Airways
91 Avenue des Champs-Elysées
Paris
☎ (1)7781414

British Caledonian Airways
Gatwick Airport
Horley
Surrey
☎ (01) 668 4222

British Midland Airways
East Midlands Airport
Castle Donington
Derbyshire
☎ (0332) 810552

Continental Shipping (SNCM)
179 Piccadilly
London W1V 9DB
☎ (01) 4914968

French Railways (SNCF)
179 Piccadilly
London W1V 0BA
☎ (01) 4093418

Pan Am
200 Mamoroneck Ave
White Plains
New York
☎ (800) 2211111

Pan Am
35 Rue Pastorelli
Nice
☎ (93) 809988

Pan Am
1 Rue Scribe
75009 Paris
☎ (1) 2664545

Pan Am
46 Via Bissolati
Rome
Italy

Sogedis Voyages (Italy to Corsica
  Ferries)
BP 239
20294 Bastia
☎ 95311809

TAT (Air Travel)
17 Rue de la Paix
75002 Paris
☎ (1) 42618585

Tourist Information

Agence Régionale du Tourisme
  et des Loisirs de Corse
22 Cours Grandval
20176 Ajaccio
☎ 95510022

Délégation Régionale du Tourisme
38 Cours Napoléon BP 162
20178 Ajaccio
☎ 95215531

Direction Régionale des Affaires
  Culturelles
19 Cours Napoléon
20176 Ajaccio
☎ 95217027

French Government Tourist Office
9401 Wilshire Boulevard
Suite 640
Beverly Hills
California 90212
☎ (213) 2712665/2722661

French Government Tourist Office
645 North Michigan Avenue
Suite 630
Chicago
Illinois 60611
☎ (312) 3376301

French Government Tourist Office
World Trade Centre 103
2050 Stemmons Freeway
P.O. Box 58610
Dallas
Texas 75258
☎ (214) 7427011

French Government Tourist Office
178 Piccadilly
London W1V 0AL
☎ (01) 491 7622 0891 244123

French Government Tourist Office
610 Fifth Ave
New York
NY 10020
☎ (212) 9571125

French Government Tourist Office
One-Halladie Plaza
Suite 250
San Francisco
California 94102
☎ (415) 9864161

Maison du Tourisme Corse
12 Rue Godot de Mauroy
75009 Paris
☎ (1) 7420434

Paris-Corse Accueil
3 Rue des Lavandières
Ste-Opportune
75001 Paris
☎(1) 42362329

Vehicle Hire

Bicycles/Mopeds
Antoniotti G.
Ile Rousse
Av des Allées
☎ 95600262

Avis
Hôtel Marina Viva
20166 Porticcio
☎ 95250315

Balagne Cycles
2 Résidence Laniella
Calvi
☎ 95651244

Locacycles
40 Boulevard Campinchi
Bastia
☎ 95390335

Locanautic
Campo dell' Oro Airport

Boats
Centre Nautique Marine
 de Bonifacio
Bonifacio
☎ 95730313

Corsica Yachting
Port de Plaisance
Propriano
☎ 95760929

Locazur
Golfe Juan
Quai de la Citadelle
Ajaccio
☎ 95221405

Raffin Marine
La Marine
Porto-Vecchio
☎ 95701330

Caravans/Campers
Citer
Société Citroën
RN 193
Bastia
☎ 95314209

Cars
(Full list available from the French
Government Tourist office)

Avis
3 Place de Gaulle
Ajaccio
☎ 95210186
or
Route de Mezzavia
Ajaccio
☎ 95221944
or
Airport, Ajaccio
☎ 95232514
or
2 Rue Notre-Dame de Lourdes
Bastia
☎ 95325730

Hertz
8 Cours Grandval
Ajaccio
☎ 95217094
or
Airport, Ajaccio
☎ 95232417
or
Casa Nostra
Quartier Giambelli
Bastia
☎ 95312749

Help in Corsica

Air Corse, Ajaccio Airport
  ☎ 95206130
Ambulance ☎ 18
Coach Travel:
  Ajaccio ☎ 95212801
  Ile Rousse ☎ 95211408
Corse Aéro Service
  Ajaccio ☎ 95232142
  Propriano ☎ 95760499
Diving emergencies ☎ 95215267
  (Haute-Corse)
Emergency Medical Service
  (SAMU) ☎ 95215050
Fire ☎ 18
Gendarmerie (Ajaccio) ☎ 9523203
          (Bastia) ☎ 95335206

Hospitals:
Ajaccio, Centre Hospitalier, Av
  Impératrice-Eugénie
  ☎ 95219090
Bastia, Centre Hospitalier
  ☎ 95319915
Calvi, Antenne Médicale, SMUR
  Ancien Presbytère ☎ 95651122
Corte, Hôpital Civil, La Gare
  ☎ 95460136
Porto-Vecchio, Antenne Médicale
  ☎ 95770005
Sartène Hôpital ☎ 95770426
Mountain region information
(skiing, accommodation, etc):
  Asco ☎ 95478207
  Bastelica ☎ 95287061
  Col de Vergio ☎ 95480105
  Ghisoni ☎ 95576128
  Quenza ☎ 95786211
  Soccia ☎ 95283167
  Zicavo ☎ 95244005
Mountain rescue ☎ 95233031
Mountain weather forecast
  ☎ 95201224/95360524
Poisoning emergency (Haute-
  Corse) ☎ 95752525
Police Station (Haute-Corse)
  ☎ 95335206
Police ☎ 17
Stations:
  Ajaccio ☎ 95231103
  Bastia ☎ 95326006
  Calvi ☎ 95650061
  Ponte-Lecchia ☎ 95477612
Taxis:
  Ajaccio   ☎ 95212814
            ☎ 95210087
            ☎ 95232570
  Bastia   ☎ 95310302
  Porto-
  Vecchio   ☎ 95700849
  Propriano ☎ 95760458
Weather forecast:
  Corse-du-Sud ☎ 95213271
  Haute-Corse ☎ 95360496

INDEX

Index to Places

Index to Subjects